A WANDER
THROUGH
WARTIME
LONDON

A WANDER THROUGH WARTIME LONDON

Five Walks Revisiting the Blitz

by

Clive Harris and Neil Bright

Pen & Sword
MILITARY

First published in Great Britain in 2010 by
Pen & Sword Military
an imprint of
Pen & Sword Books Ltd
47 Church Street
Barnsley
South Yorkshire
S70 2AS

ISBN 978 1 84884 172 7

A CIP catalogue record for this book is
available from the British Library

Typeset in Sabon by
Phoenix Typesetting, Auldgirth, Dumfriesshire

Printed and bound in England by
CPI UK

Pen & Sword Books Ltd incorporates the Imprints of Pen & Sword
Aviation, Pen & Sword Maritime, Pen & Sword Military, Wharncliffe
Local History, Pen & Sword Select, Pen & Sword Military Classics, Leo
Cooper, Remember When, Seaforth Publishing and Frontline Publishing.

For a complete list of Pen & Sword titles please contact
PEN & SWORD BOOKS LIMITED
47 Church Street, Barnsley, South Yorkshire, S70 2AS, England
E-mail: enquiries@pen-and-sword.co.uk
Website: www.pen-and-sword.co.uk

This book is dedicated to all those Londoners who persevered through adversity to write a dramatic chapter in this city's great history but specifically the memory of

Pat Bright,
A devoted mother and fire watcher

&

Charles Peter Miller,
Grandfather & ARP warden

Contents

Preface

Redundancy in 1992 led me to hastily arrange some First World War battlefield trips in addition to several trips already organised. The guide on the first trip was none other than Clive Harris, my co-author. We quite quickly struck up a friendship. I think it was initially because I am from South London and Clive wished he was! Joking aside Clive told me he was close to having his first book, *Walking the London Blitz*, published and that, as a Londoner, I should research my area in that period. I became more and more fascinated by the Blitz. Living in Southwark it was quickly apparent that the area was in the front line and despite my parents telling me some of their stories, I did not realize the scale of devastation and loss of life involved.

Many hours of research followed, as did talks and walks and now this volume. I am never ceased to be amazed when I hear new stories of the Blitz. In writing this many people have given up their precious time to help with the research and have plodded the streets of Southwark with me. I would naturally like to thank Clive, for his great help, true friendship and unceasing enthusiasm on any battlefield. Many thanks go to Steve Hunnisett for a tremendous amount of encouragement, his toil in many archive centres, pounding the beat and great friendship. Local historian, Stephen Humphrey, has been fantastically helpful as have Steve Potter and the staff of Southwark Local Studies Library and London Metropolitan Archives. Greenwich Heritage has also been wonderfully helpful. I would also like to thank walkers; Michele and Richard Page Jones, Marietta Crichton Stuart, Mike Garbett, Peter and Alison Campbell, Maurice Klingels and Andy Pepper. Please excuse me if I have left omitted you. You are all fantastic.

Lastly and most importantly I would like to thank my lovely wife, Tracey. She is my rock, chauffeur and my dearest friend.

Neil Bright, Southwark 2010

A faded piece of paper in my Grandfather's drawer was uncovered after his death;

"Dear Sir, I have received a letter signed by a large number of people living in Green End and Hawkshead Roads asking me to convey their thanks for all those who gave help at the occurrence in Green End Road on Saturday 19 April 1941. Particular reference is made to the valuable work you did before the official parties arrived and I am accordingly glad to be able to tell you how much your assistance was appreciated by the people concerned.

Yours Faithfully, H. Lockyer (Town Clerk and ARP Controller)

He had never spoken of it but my Grandfather, Charles Peter Miller, then just 18, had played his part in London's story during the last war. I feel that that story is also mine, through fortune of post war migration I grew up as a bona fide "Mockney" and proud of it, Welwyn Garden City my home and South & West London my roots. Some relatives did speak of the war and those dinner table reminiscences inspired me to discover more. In 2002, when I wrote *Walking the London Blitz*, I asked readers to "find the last rusty curtain hooks of the war before they disappeared forever". Thankfully that statement was premature and researching this book turned up more remaining reminders than I could have ever imagined. My thanks must go to Neil who worked tirelessly to traipse the streets of his native South London to bring his neighbourhood's history to life again, fellow Addick and friend Steve Hunnisett who went above and beyond the call of duty in his assistance with the book, my mates Dave Saunders, John Mogie and Julian Whippy for walking the walks and enduring my endless talk of London's war, my family, as ever, played their part from son Georgie Addam, now four years old but already a keen historian to my soul mate Ali, my beautiful blue, for her love and loyalty throughout and finally my father Brian, who has shown us all, and himself, that some things in life are worth fighting for. I am very proud to call him *my Dad* and love him very much.

Clive Harris, "Highwood" Knebworth 2010

Introduction
by Steve Hunnisett

Although this book deals principally with the German attacks on London during the Second World War, London had suffered previous air attacks. During The Great War, London had been subjected to bombing raids by airships and Gotha bombers sporadically from 1915 to 1917. During these raids, just over 2,900 people had been killed or injured and these raids, coupled with those during the Spanish Civil War, gave the planners food for thought when predicting the anticipated casualties of any raids on British cities during a future conflict. As a result, very doom laden forecasts were made in 1938 that 1,800,000 civilians would be killed or wounded in Britain during the opening six months of any future war.

As events were later to prove, these estimates were far too pessimistic and the final total of deaths resulting from enemy air attacks was only a tiny fraction of those originally predicted.

The threat of bombing became real once France had fallen in June 1940 as this gave the opportunity for the Luftwaffe to use captured French and Belgian airfields, thus bringing London and most other British cities within range. From July to September, the Germans concentrated resources on bombing the RAF's airfields as a prelude to an invasion planned for the autumn of 1940 and London was declared 'off limits' by Hitler, who still had hopes that Britain would be forced into peace negotiations.

However, as with many events in wartime, the London Blitz came about as a result of a mistake – on 24 August 1940, some German bombers, whose original target was Shellhaven in the Thames Estuary, became lost due to a navigational error and jettisoned their bombs not over open countryside as intended but over London, falling on the City of London and parts of East and North London. In retaliation, Churchill ordered a raid by the RAF on Berlin and although Bomber Command's aircraft of the time could barely carry a worthwhile bomb load over that range, the loss of face in Germany was enormous. After all, Goering had boasted that no enemy aircraft would fly over Reich territory and as a result of this raid, Hitler ordered the Luftwaffe to turn its attention to full scale attacks on London. Ironically, this took the pressure off Fighter Command and effectively ensured German defeat in the Battle of Britain, thus precluding any serious chance of an invasion of Britain.

The periods when London was under attack fall into four distinct phases:

The First or Night Blitz

The first mass raid was on 'Black Saturday' 7 September 1940 when German bombers hit targets concentrated around the Port of London. This was the first of fifty-seven consecutive nights when London was bombed and although there were later some attack-free nights, this phase continued until the night of 10/11 May 1941 when the largest raid proved to be the last for some months as the Germans shifted resources in readiness for their attack on Russia.

The Baedecker Raids

In retaliation for the RAF's bombing of Lubeck in March 1942, Hitler ordered raids on Britain's historic cities and to select targets, the Luftwaffe planners reputedly used the Baedecker Tourist Guides, thus making Canterbury, Exeter, York, Norwich, Bath and London on a small scale the principal targets. These raids lasted for a short time between April and June 1942 and were nowhere near the same scale or intensity of the First Blitz.

The Baby Blitz

Operation Steinbock, to use its correct title, was the next phase, which commenced in December 1943. Once again, these raids were not of the same scale as before and the vastly improved defences ensured that this operation ended by May 1944. It was a resounding defeat for the Luftwaffe, who lost many aircraft and crews who would be sorely missed when the Allies invaded Europe in June 1944.

The Terror Weapons

On 13 June 1944, barely a week after D-Day, the first V-1 Flying Bomb fell on Grove Road Railway Bridge in Bow, East London. In the coming months, over 9,000 of these weapons were launched from ramped sites in France, but of those launched some 6,500 were brought down by Anti-Aircraft gunfire, by the balloon barrage and by the Spitfire and Tempest fighters of the RAF. However, some 2,500 did get through to London, bringing further death and destruction to the capital city. On 8 September 1944, worse was to come when the first V-2 long range rocket landed in Chiswick, West London. These were truly terrifying weapons against which there was no defence. Gradually though, the V-1's launch sites were overrun by the advancing Allied armies and the V-2's mobile launchers were gradually forced out of range. The final V-2 fell on Orpington, Kent on 27 March 1945 and the final V-1 fell on open countryside in Hertfordshire two days later.

Around 60,000 civilians had been killed by enemy air attack across the UK, about half of them in the capital city, but London was finally safe again.

Published Sources:
The Narrow Margin – Derek Wood with Derek Dempster, Tri Service Press 1969
The Most Dangerous Enemy – Stephen Bungay, Aurum Press 2000
Walking the London Blitz – Clive Harris, Pen & Sword 2003
The City That Wouldn't Die – Richard Collier, Collins 1959

Chapter One

Blackheath to Greenwich

Start point – Blackheath Station (direct trains can be reached
from London Bridge & Waterloo East)
End point – Greenwich Station (DLR or overland service back
to London Bridge & Waterloo East)
Duration of Walk – 3/4 hours

On exiting Blackheath Station (which can be busy when a lively
farmers' market takes place on Sundays), turn left and walk to
All Saints Church where our walk begins on the edge of the
heath.

Construction of All Saints Church began in 1857 and took
ten years to complete. Its architect, Benjamin Ferrey, chose
sturdy Kentish rag stone surfaces and by the time war came A.
W. Blomfield had added the vestries and porch to the original
design. The spire is also a later edition dating back to 1899 –
prior to that the church had rather unkindly been referred to as
the "Kentish Barns". The church survived the war but bears the
scars of several near misses; a number of windows were
damaged by blast but more obvious damage can be found at the
entrance where the railings have been taken away as part of
the war effort (a common sacrifice the length and breadth of the
country), there is little evidence that they later became Spitfires!
Another impact on the congregation was the loss of three vicars
during the war years; the first joined his family who had evacuated, the second was removed and the third to a nervous
breakdown.

When stood outside, the great expanse of Blackheath draws
your attention. We shall return to it later, however, so for now
head due south towards Royal Parade to the junction with

WALK I - BLACKHEATH TO GREENWICH

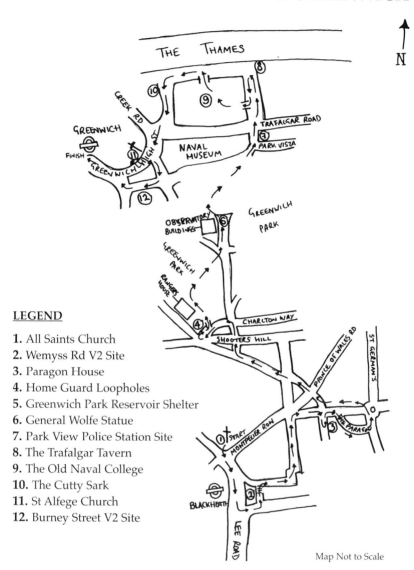

LEGEND

1. All Saints Church
2. Wemyss Rd V2 Site
3. Paragon House
4. Home Guard Loopholes
5. Greenwich Park Reservoir Shelter
6. General Wolfe Statue
7. Park View Police Station Site
8. The Trafalgar Tavern
9. The Old Naval College
10. The Cutty Sark
11. St Alfege Church
12. Burney Street V2 Site

Map Not to Scale

Tranquil Vale. This parade was severely damaged towards the end of the war when local lad Bob Land remembers;

> *"On another occasion, towards the end of the war, there had been extensive damage to a few shops in Tranquil Vale, and having taken my Grandmother's broom, I helped the fire brigade sweep up the glass which was lying on the pavement from all the shattered shop windows. I can still recall the smell of charred timbers, iodine and broken plaster board"*

On the west side of the road can be found a splendid arts and crafts church hall constructed in the 1920s. It replaces the original building on this site that was damaged in an air raid in the Great War.

On 24 August 1916 (wrongly captioned the 14th on the

HOUSE IN TRANQUIL VALE, BLACKHEATH VILLAGE, THE MORNING AFTER THE ZEPPELIN RAID, AUGUST 14TH, 1916.
N.B.—FIREMAN AT WORK IN WINDOW FRAME.
SITE NOW OCCUPIED BY ALL SAINTS' CHURCH HALL.

The Blackheath Airship Raid - note the incorrect date, no raid took place on this day

displayed photograph), thirteen Naval Airships headed for London. One of them, L31 captained by Heinrich Mathy, used skilful flying and low cloud to get himself over south east London. His six-engine Zeppelin, with a top speed of 64mph, was also carrying a pay load of 240lb bombs, at the time the heaviest the world had known.

Mathy, who was by the time of the raid a household name in Britain due to his feared bombing airship exploits, managed to drop thirty-six bombs in nine minutes. In total forty-nine people were killed and a further forty wounded, including twenty-three men of No2 HT Depot Army Service Corps who were billeted in the area. In total £130,000 of damage was caused in the raid, no small sum for the day. Though the airship left Britain unscathed, it suffered a heavy landing and was damaged for some weeks. L31 and Mathy would meet their own end just months later when shot down by 2/Lt Tempest over Potters Bar in early October of the same year.

Leaving the scene of this historic event head back towards the railway station in Blackheath village. Opposite its entrance you will see Blackheath Grove. Turn left and then left again into a car park behind the parade of shops.

In 1945 this was the site of a Wesleyan Chapel. On the evening of 8 March a V2 struck this very spot killing five people and wounding 134. The damage caused was severe; it was reported that not a single window in Blackheath Village remained unbroken. Even a train that was stopped at Blackheath Station at the time of the explosion had windows damaged. The 13-ton rocket arrived at 3,000 miles per hour straight out of the stratosphere; it was one of twelve to land in the borough of Lewisham between September 1945 and March 1945. In this incident four people were to lose their lives, one of those, sixty-four-year-old Albert Brown, was a fire watcher and ARP local warden. He was in No 14 Montpelier Vale when the rocket struck; taken to Lewisham Hospital, wounded in the incident, he passed away on 4 June 1945 almost a month after VE Day. Given the time and day the rocket struck, though tragic, these casualties were relatively light when compared to the 168 who lost their lives when a V2 struck the Woolworth's in New Cross Gate in the previous November.

A good comparison can be made by lining up the church spire

The aftermath of the Wemyss Road Incident, total devastation

of All Saints in the contemporary photograph shown. Leave this solemn spot via the stairs ahead of you that lead up onto Wemyss Road and turn right. This short road shows battle scars from the V2 on both sides of the street, notably the right-hand side, and is dominated by the imposing Blackheath High School for girls.

The school, opened in 1885 by Princess Louise, was one of a number across the country founded by the Girls Public Day School Company to provide education for girls that equalled public schools for boys. War was no stranger to the schools as in the 1914–1918 war extra curriculum activities included the knitting of socks and comforts for the troops overseas alongside the provision of food parcels. The older students and staff also volunteered to work in nearby factories making compasses for aircraft at the weekends. The playing fields were turned into allotments to assist the war effort before being requisitioned by the army in 1916. In 1939, however, the threat was a lot closer to home and a decision was made as early as 1938 to evacuate pupils and staff to Tonbridge Wells High School. Within days of war being declared the Wemyss Road facility was almost empty leaving just a skeleton staff to maintain the building, and staff and pupils were settling down to a new life in Kent. By July 1944 the school relocated to Taunton due to the V1 flight paths being directly over Tonbridge Wells. By the following spring the Allies were pushing deeper into Europe, bringing nearer the end of the war and a return to Blackheath. When the V2 struck considerable damage was caused to the building. Though peace came within weeks, the summer holidays were spent by ex pupils, staff and local families clearing debris and making good the repairs so that school life could return in the autumn of 1945. The building remains a girl's school today and the scars of war appear to have healed.

We turn left into Paragon Place and pause outside No3. Though the building itself was not damaged it was the home of Mrs Winifred Adams, a nursing sister in charge of the First Aid Post in Westhorne Avenue, Eltham. These FAPs were an essential link in the civil defences, often providing primary care for those wounded during raids and placing their own lives in danger to treat others. The post took a direct hit on the night of 15 March 1941 when three nurses, including Winifred, three first aid attendants and three patients were killed. At the top of the road we arrive on the fringe of Blackheath once more and turn right onto South Row.

A mixture of new and old architecture marks a stretch of buildings at the end of Montpellier Row. Its eclectic nature is the result of a raid on 19 March 1941. This date opened the beginning of the Luftwaffe 'Spring Offensive' over Britain and became known infamously locally as 'the Saturday'. In total 479 aircraft dropped 470 tons of HE and 122,000 incendiary bombs on the capital, though the main target on this night were the docks east of London Bridge. Both South East London and the East End suffered the worst night's bombing since October in a raid that lasted from just after 2000hrs to 0200hrs the following morning. Casualties that night were particularly high with 631 Londoner's losing their lives. A number of incidents were reported in this area and the photographs show a comparison of the building in South Row before the raid and just before their demolition.

South Row before the war

After a short stroll along their frontage we turn right into Pond Road. The first imposing building on the left is Paragon House; it was severely damaged on the night of 16 April 1941.

This date saw another major raid on the capital. Between 2050hrs and 0520hrs some 685 aircraft delivered 890 tons of

The same houses 'blitzed' in 1944

Paragon House after the bombings

HE and dropped over 151,000 incendiary bombs. Many crews flew two and even three bombing missions over London from their air bases in France and Belgium. Originally LC50 Parachute flares were dropped to locate the target areas concentrated along the banks of the Thames downstream of Tower Bridge. Later large fires from Rotherhithe Gas Works, Surrey Commercial Docks and Stepney Power Station acted as boundary markers for the raiding aircraft.

At the height of the raid, German crews were reporting up to eighty conflagrations; in this corner of Blackheath the local civil defences were on the verge of being overwhelmed by the sheer number of incidents. The nearest AFS crews were stations 46W at Charlton Manor School, Nigeria Road and 43X, located in the Rangers House just across the heath, who were unable to prevent major superficial damage to the house. The comparison photographs of this building present a fascinating glimpse of the damage suffered by residential properties around this time.

The raid on 16 April 1941 was a retaliatory bombing for the damage caused to the Berlin State Opera house by the RAF on the 9 April. It was ominously prophesied by Lord Haw Haw (William Joyce) who announced "There's going to be a bombing" on his 'Germany Calling' programme broadcast on Deutschlandsender Radio in Hamburg. Though a subject of ridicule and mockery to many people listening, during this period of the Blitz he often promised these major air raids with alarming accuracy.

Returning to South Row we turn right and head into The Paragon. This impressive row of Georgian Town Houses was built between 1795 and 1806. Intended for the upper middle class, the linked pairs of houses provided room for carriages, stables, servant's quarters and large gardens. By 1914 many had been converted into hotels and boarding houses. As you enter you will note the Festival of Britain Award for Merit Plaque awarded in 1951 on the right-hand house, now extremely rare items to find. This one also commemorates the completion of the post-war repairs on these historic buildings. First damaged when an HE landed onto the back basement of No3 on 19

The Paragon partially destroyed

Gaps in the Paragon, 1941

October 1940 just after midnight, the dates 16 and 19 April play heavily in the wartime story of the Paragon. At No8/10 two people lost their lives when the building took a direct hit and further along the row the comparison photographs show the damage caused prior to their rebuilding between 1949/51; only a veteran post box remains bearing the scars of that night's raid. A V1 rocket also caused severe damage when it struck No1 at the junction with Morden Path on 3 July 1944. In this incident there was one fatal casualty though another ten people were omitted to hospital.

After rebuilding was completed, the Paragon, an important glimpse of our Georgian past was converted into residential apartments, as they remain to this day.

We return to South Row and take the footpath across to the Heath heading towards Prince of Wales Road, before crossing the road. Note the Prince of Wales Pond that fronts the end of Montpellier Row. It existed prior to the war being marked on the 1894 Ordnance Survey map and is described in 1944 by local resident Rosemary Radley who was just a small girl when she recalled;

'The Heath was and still is a much-frequented place of leisure: boys and dads kicking footballs and flying kites; girls playing "he"; parents and children picnicking on the grass and sailing boats on the pond near the Princess of Wales public house in Pond Road. There was tremendous buzz on the Heath.'

No doubt that the pond, in addition to providing youngsters with a boating facility, also assisted the AFS crews with a ready supply of water should it be required. A good view of the pond before the war can be seen in the photographs of South Row.

To the east of us is a row of large houses known as St Germans Place. St Germans Church nearby was totally destroyed by two flying bomb incidents in July 1944; it had already been damaged in 1940. Rosemary Radley, talking of her experiences in 1944, wrote;

'Our church was St German's, an elegant Georgian building overlooking the Heath, with white walls without and blue and gold fittings within, built in the same period as the elegant houses on the other side of the Heath. Canon Galer was the Rector. My parents were not great churchgoers, but they sent me to the Sunday school attached to St German's. A land mine completely destroyed our church, St German's in St German's Place, very close to our house. That was in June 1944. Ironic, nicht wahr, that it should have been the Germans who bombed the church dedicated to St Germanus? I may have been only 4¾ but the bombing of St German's church made an impression on my mind.

But what a shock when next morning we came downstairs to breakfast after the bombing to behold our solid wooden front door blasted off its hinges. The door was blown inwards and lay in the hall, revealing an empty doorway open to the elements, broken glass everywhere. We had to step gingerly over it to get to breakfast. The door was nailed back into place in a temporarily permanent fashion, but for quite a time it was unopenable, that is, until the War Damage Commission people came round. The instruction given was that the back door only was to be used, but when I got back from school it was all too easy to forget the new drill. I would blithely knock on the front door to be let in, only to be told off for not remembering!

The destruction of St German's church was sad. Like our front door, the church was unusable, but we did get our front door back. Alas, we didn't get our church back! For a long time the church lay in ruins, to be replaced some time later by an insensitively designed block of flats, which sticks out like a sore thumb in a row of Georgian houses. What a travesty! But it has to be admitted that with so many churches in Blackheath, the bombing of St German's has done the Diocese of Southwark a good turn in the long run.'

The incident logs for the borough show no mention of a parachute mine in June 1944 but two V1 strikes in the following month. Also affected by this incident were Ambulance Station 126 located in Christ's College in St Germans Place and the Fire station in Liskard Gardens.

Crossing the road we are now on the Heath itself, a historic site that was the rallying point for Wat Tyler's peasant's revolt of 1381. Seventy years later the 1450 Kentish Rebellion, led by

Anti invasion defences on Blackheath

Jack Cade, also started here and the Cornish Rebels were defeated here in 1497 in what became known as 'The Battle of Deptford Bridge'. In the seventeenth century highwaymen plied their trade on the main coach routes to Dover nearby and the 1878 Guidebook *Walfords Old & New London* graphically described the heath;

> *"In past times it was planted with gibbets, on which the bleaching bones of men who had dared to ask for some extension of liberty, or who doubted the infallibility of kings, were left year after year to dangle in the wind."*

By 1939 the heath was gearing up for an even more dramatic scene, it was utilised for numerous military uses throughout the war years, the first being the construction of anti-glider defences during the threat of invasion in 1940. Piles of earth were dug at intervals to deter this threat as the photograph uncovered in Greenwich Archives clearly shows. We will head across Blackheath via Long Pond Road and Duke Humphrey Road footpaths aiming for the main gates to Greenwich Park.

Anti invasion defences on Blackheath

The Heath today, a popular spot for picnics, kiting and football, was the spot where legendary English cricketer Colin Blythe first picked up a ball whilst on holiday from the Woolwich Arsenal. A fine bowler who was in the successful pre-war Kent county side, he met an untimely end in the Ypres Salient in 1917 whilst serving with the King's Own Yorkshire Light Infantry. Throughout the early war years the use of the heath intensified for military purposes. Anti-aircraft guns, barrage balloons and searchlight batteries cropped up on the heath.

After the threat of invasion passed a hutted prisoner of war camp was also established here that remained post war. A relative recalls them being allowed to watch Charlton play at the Valley in the winter of 1947. They had cleared the pitch of snow prior to kick off and were given their own section of the vast east terrace. The game had to be stopped following a very one-sided snowball fight with 40,000 local football supporters and the Germans were marched back to their huts on Blackheath for their own safety!

In total, seven V1 rockets and a V2 landed onto the Heath during the war alongside numerous craters appearing from conventional bombs. The holes were filled in after the war with debris from Blitz damaged buildings and this in turn led to a bad case of subsidence in 2002 that led to emergency road works causing problems for motorists crossing the Heath.

At the entrance to Greenwich Park, known as the Blackheath Gate, follow the high park brick wall west along Charlton Road to its corner opposite the Keepers Lodge house. Here you will find purpose built loopholes in the brickwork. This was the work of the local defence Volunteers, more commonly known as The Home Guard; the local detachment was raised in July 1940 as the 25th Battalion London Home Guard, split into No16 Greenwich Company under Col Newington and No14 Blackheath Company under Major Thorne, whose house in Blackheath became HQ, recruiting centre and dining room for the unit. By 13 July, after a stringent interview process to enlist, forty-eight men paraded on Blackheath, all had even been issued with rifles. Rifle instruction was provided by some local regular army NCOs on the open space SW of Brook Hospital.

On 19 March 1941, Squad Leader Leonard Matthews became an early casualty during a raid whilst fire-fighting. The

Home guard loopholes in the wall of Greenwich Park

sixty-three-year-old initially lost a leg when a bomb landed nearby; he died of his wounds a week later. A great loss to the unit, Leonard Matthews had served as a sergeant in the Great War with the Army Service Corps, he had served in France and Malta where he had contracted malaria and dysentery before being invalided out of the army with a rib injury in 1918.

The main role of the unit can be viewed from the corner of the park wall. Behind an often locked park keeper's gate was a strongpoint constructed by the unit during those early days; with the threat of invasion came preparations to defend the East/West arterial road that runs across the park, Charlton Way. Tanks were expected to strike into the heart of the capital across this ground so with a Bren gun team and observer situated in the upper floors of the Keepers Lodge, in front of Folly Pond, the main body of troops could man the loopholes to stop the invader in his tracks. It seems almost incredulous today but in 1940 this was a very real threat and a very simple but serious solution to fight on by the Home Guard. One evening a volunteer party of eighteen men were requested for all night duty at this strong point ninety-three men turned up for the parade. A lucky escape occurred when a HE bomb landed outside the Keepers Lodge just after midnight on the 18 September 1940.

Though detonated it landed on the grass verge and caused no damage or casualties.

On another occasion when an RAF fighter was shot down over Blackheath, it crashed to the west of the Heath near to Holly Hedge House. The pilot, whilst parachuting to safety, was strafed by a German pilot, his body falling lifeless into a garden in Shooters Hill. The Home Guard recovered it and guarded the pilot's remains and aircraft overnight until the authorities arrived. No14 Company drill hall was badly bombed in April 1941, thankfully with no loss of life. The same night nearby Holly Hedge House, a Territorial Barracks on the western edge of the Heath was also destroyed. This impressive mansion house constructed in the eighteenth century for the Vicar of Lewisham had long been the headquarters of the 20th Battalion London Regiment and recruiting centre in both wars. It was pulled down in 1946 due to the irreparable bomb damage; a modern TA Centre was established and is still visible on the site today.

We retrace our steps and enter Greenwich Park via the first pedestrian entrance encountered off Charlton Way; the rose garden ahead is located at the rear of an impressive building known as The Rangers House. This was the site of AFS station 43X. The house itself suffered substantial damage during the war and shrapnel scars are visible, notably on 21 September 1940 at around 2200hrs when three delayed action bombs fell in the vicinity. The first damaged the bowling green, the second the tennis courts and the third the main building itself. On the following night a bomb struck the gas main in the building. It exploded but luckily the AFS crews were on hand to prevent too much further damage.

We now head due east towards the centre of the park. Before long a large raised covered reservoir comes into view. This area was utilized as a public shelter known as Air Raid Shelter No4, originally the property of Kent Water Works. It was damaged on the night of 21 September when first a HE bomb landed just twenty-five yards south of the shelter; no casualties were reported. The following afternoon a suspected delayed action bomb was found on the site of Crooms Hill Tumuli, around 150 yards from the shelter. This was one of a number of 'strange' items being discovered around the area reported as delayed action bombs at this time as the Luftwaffe found more

The entrance to Greenwich Park Air Raid Shelter

ingenious weapons to drop on London. The occupants of No 40 Grove Street reported a UXB in their front room; on arrival civil defence workers found it to be a nose cone from an anti-aircraft shell that had dropped through the front window. More of a threat was the '4 foot long metal cylinder attached by wires to a cylindrical object' discovered 200 yards from the main entrance to Greenwich Park on 2 November 1940. It turned out to be a flare fuse attached to a flare container and the first of its kind to be found intact.

On reaching Great Cross Avenue within the park head north towards the Royal Observatory buildings and stop by the Altazimuth building. Dating from 1899 it is named after the original telescope that was housed in its dome. The building was damaged when a HE Bomb landed just 150 yards away, on 8 December 1940. Windows were blown in, the thin skin of the dome shattered and the entrance destroyed, though luckily no one was injured. The precious telescope was blown from its

The sorry looking Altazimuth building after a raid

mounting during this raid and much repair work was needed to make it workable once more.

Damage to the park was not uncommon with a total thirty plus incidents recorded within its grounds during the war. Also close to this spot is the General Wolfe memorial, and from this spot tourists and locals alike stand in awe over the sight of London spreading out before you. A truly great viewpoint of the capital, it did not survive unscathed. On the south side the scars of war are easily visible from a bomb that landed on 25 October 1940. Landing just east of this spot it struck at 1500hrs whilst people were out strolling and taking in the views. Thankfully there are no recorded casualties in this incident. Two V1 rockets fell within the park grounds, firstly on 15 July 1944 at 1358 one landed somewhat harmlessly just 50m from the Wolfe memorial causing little damage, secondly in the flower bed near to the Vanburgh Park gate on 31 July 1944 a lone walker was taken to hospital when a rocket struck at 1815hrs.

We now walk down the hill towards the Naval College

aiming for the Park Row exit. Proceed down Park Row and take care when crossing the busy Trafalgar Road. Look back to the corner building of Park Row behind you; this was the site of Park Row Police Station. A V1 Rocket landed on the police station just after midnight on 8 July 1944. The building suffered extensive damage, and there were eight minor casualties including three police officers. In the station occurrence book it refers to a number of the casualties as being 'visitors'. It is interesting to note that the cells suffered the most damage! It had already suffered bomb damage during the night 10/11 May 1941, the heaviest night's raiding on London in the war. On this occasion a bomb dropped onto the adjacent Queen Public

A young looking Steve Hunnisett in front of a shrapnel-scarred Wolfe Memorial

Park Row Police Station during the Great War

House destroying the pub and damaging the police station. Two casualties were evacuated to the nearby Millers Hospital.

We continue toward the river along Park Row and enter the old Naval College Grounds, now a music college. At the end of the road is the Trafalgar Hotel; this famous old pub was once the haunt of MPs who would travel from Parliament to enjoy the oysters served there. On 12 September it suffered fire damage along with the Naval College buildings after a number of incendiary bombs landed in the area. Further damage to the pub was caused once more by incendiary bombs on 19 March 1941 when the fire services responded to a large fire on the premises. Adjacent to the pub in Park Row can be found a garage block; in wartime this was the home for London Auxiliary Ambulance Station TS1. Two of the rooms in the Trafalgar Tavern itself were allocated for on duty staff and admin offices.

The area around the gate you are entering was disrupted on

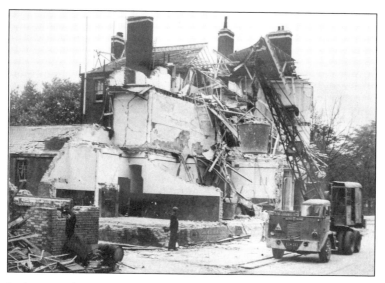

Park Row Police Station after the Blitz

the same evening by a number of delayed action bombs that landed in the vicinity. All were dealt with by bomb disposal teams before they exploded. The college grounds were hit on numerous occasions. One of the more novel incidents occurred on 13 October 1940 when a barrage balloon broke free from its cable and came to rest in the main quadrant. Fortunately an RAF team were on scene to deal with the rogue balloon before further damage could be caused. On 8 September the King Charles block was damaged by a high explosive device blowing in windows. Just twenty-four hours after the first raids on London began one special visitor to inspect the damage was Winston Churchill. During 1943 raiders returned over the skies of south east London following a break of over a year. On Wednesday, 20 January a number of low level flying Focke Wulf 190s carrying HE bombs appeared almost without warning. For reasons disputed to this day the capital's balloon defences were temporarily down and the twenty or so aircraft struck with devastation, dropping their 1,100lb bombs and strafing roads. The President's House in the Royal Naval College was hit killing one naval officer and narrowly missing the college commander. It then strafed a number of Greenwich

Churchill inspects damage to the Naval College

streets nearby with witnesses claiming that they 'could see the pilot in one plane laughing as he gunned up the tram yard'.

Head down on to the river front and turn left. Before long you pass the Bellot Obelisk; this memorial commemorates the popular French explorer Joseph Bellot, sometimes known as the Eskimos' friend. He participated in two separate expeditions to find the English explorer Sir John Franklin who had gone missing when trying to force his way through the North West Passage.

Bellot was himself killed when he slipped under the ice in the Wellington Channel in 1853 and this memorial was paid for by public subscription. The scars of war are clearly visible on it. This damage dates most likely from 8/9 December 1940 when a number of incidents were reported in the Royal Naval College grounds.

We are now on the river and it's worth pausing to consider its relevance in the air war over London. The River Thames was in many ways the origins of the city. Here where it is at its widest reaches the important industrial buildings that became vital targets for the Luftwaffe are clearly evident. To the east the London transport coal station and beyond that Siemens Cable Works were all singled out for attention. As ever the Germans would usually attack at low tide, whilst it was almost impossible to black out the river. It also offered the best supply of water to douse the fires. The water itself did not always offer respite or safety. On 19/20 March 1941 a Tug and Thames Lighter vessel was hit and sunk just offshore here with the loss of three lives.

You now enter the area around the Cutty Sark (currently undergoing major restoration following a devastating fire in 2007). This was the site of the Ship Hotel. This famous old building was first damaged on 8 September 1940 when a fire was started by incendiary bombs. Later on 1 November 1940 it was struck by a high explosive bomb. Two people were rescued from the rubble of the damaged building. It was later completely destroyed on 19/20 April 1941 and not rebuilt after the war. Also near to this spot is the entrance to the foot tunnel under the Thames. A number of incidents were recorded here.

The long since demolished Ship Hotel, now the site of the Cutty Sark

Fires were dealt with on both 8 and 23 September, and later on 1 August 1944 a flying bomb landed here at 0624hrs. The entrance to the foot tunnel was blocked and one passer-by lost their life.

Crossing Creek Road we continue up Greenwich Church Street until we arrive at St Alfege's Church. A church has been sited here since 1012 marking the spot where St Alfege, the then Archbishop of Canterbury, was murdered by Viking raiders on 19 April. In a strange quirk of history on the 929 anniversary of this date the Church was completely gutted and the roof destroyed in the heavy raid of 19 April 1941. The outer walls bear many a scar from the war; it was rebuilt as early as 1943. If the church is open it is well worth a visit as there are a number of fascinating memorials inside, notably the London Territorial Field Ambulance in the Great War as you enter on the right. One survivor of the bombings is the organ that dates to 1522, protected by its case that is still on display inside. Where possible the original wood was restored giving it the warm depth of colour seen today. General Wolfe, whose damaged statue we saw earlier in Greenwich Park, remained safe buried in the crypt beneath the church. A local primary school also bears his name. A handbook to the history of the church is

Burney Street, see how the Anderson shelters have survived the V1

The destruction of Burney Street

available in the foyer and contains a picture showing the devastation caused by the bombings.

On leaving the church we head south into Stockwell Street and then the first right into Burney Street. About halfway up on the left a flight of stairs and then an open area for parking alongside post war buildings provide us with a clue to the devastation that occurred here on 27 June 1944. Just after midnight a V1 rocket landed on the area you now stand in. Twenty-three casualties were reported, ten of which were fatal. The ton of high explosive contained in a doodlebug destroyed a number of houses. Though the devastation was tremendous the contemporary photographs taken after the incident clearly show a number of Anderson shelters intact among the rubble. We continue up Burney Street passing the modern police station and a charming memorial to Doug Mullins, a master dairyman and much loved local personality who lived on this site throughout the war years. Turn right into Royal Hill then left into Greenwich High Road where the station is found and the end of our walk.

Before finishing however one further story is worthy of note. On the left-hand side of Greenwich High Road can be found a

Stretcher fencing in East London

The sretchers in use at the Aldwych in 1944

post-war local authority block of buildings. Recently the border fence to this block was described as 'Stretcher Fencing'. Though recently replaced, a number of examples across London still exist and incredibly, as can be seen from the photographs, these fences were made up by welding wartime civil defence stretchers together to make domestic fences, and with that example of ingenious post war recycling in our thoughts our walk comes to an end.

Published Sources

i – *The Blitz Then & Now* – Winston Ramsey – After the Battle 1988

ii – *Walking the London Blitz* – Clive Harris – Pen & Sword 2003

iii – *Red Alert* – Lewis Blake – Lewis Blake 1982

iv – *The Home Guard of Britain* – Charles Graves – Hutchinson & Co 1943

v – *London Fire Service Directory of Auxiliary Sub Stations* – W.F. Hickin – The Watchroom 2000

Unpublished Sources

i – Bob Land – www.blackheathbugle.wordpress.com

ii – Rosemary Radley – BBC Website/the peoples war

iii – The Authors' family recollections

Chapter Two

The Marylebone Walk

Start Point – Tottenham Court Road Station
(Central/Northern Line)
End point – Baker Street Station
(Bakerloo/Circle/Metropolitan Line)
Duration – 3/4 hours

Our walk starts at the busy Tottenham Court Road station. This station was rebuilt in 1965 and therefore shows no obvious signs of damage. The station was, however, hit on 24 September 1940, a raid that saw an estimated 110 aircraft over the skies of the capital with civil defence groups 1, 2 and 3 (Inner London North Thames) receiving the worst of the bombings. In total seventy people lost their lives that night in London and a further 350 were wounded. One of those killed, though anonymous today, lost their life at the entrance to Tottenham Court Road station where you now stand. It is of interest to also note that the night of 24 September 1940 marked the night of the RAF's raid on Berlin in what Churchill described as a form of 'proportional retaliation'. Though many bombs are believed to have failed to detonate, including one that fell in the garden of Hitler's Chancellery, twenty-two German civilians were killed. The RAF was 'hitting back' and the air war was about to intensify. The station had been closed on the day war was declared for F.A.M. work (Flood Alleviation Measures). These preventative steps had been considered from the autumn of 1938 to stop the bombing from breaching the tunnels that run under the River Thames should war become a reality. Initially this was just a matter of plugging existing tunnels with concrete. By 1939, however, a more practical plan of remote controlled

WALK II - THE MARYLEBONE WALK

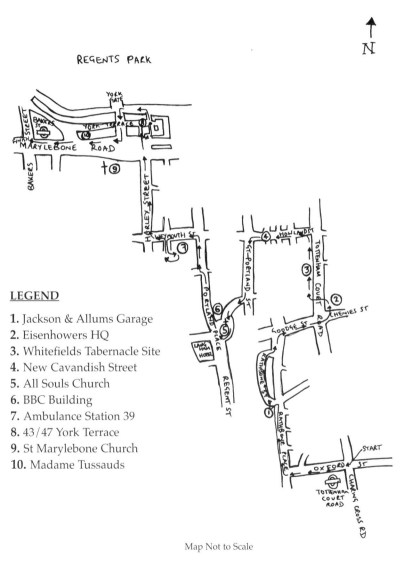

LEGEND

1. Jackson & Allums Garage
2. Eisenhowers HQ
3. Whitefields Tabernacle Site
4. New Cavandish Street
5. All Souls Church
6. BBC Building
7. Ambulance Station 39
8. 43/47 York Terrace
9. St Marylebone Church
10. Madame Tussauds

Map Not to Scale

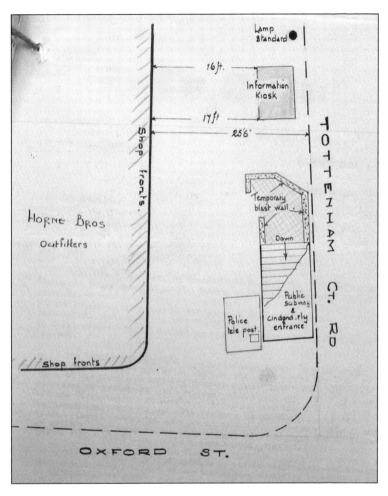

A wartime sketch of the Tottenham Court Road Station flood defences and info kiosk

flood barriers was adopted at vulnerable areas. This did prevent a full service during a raid as trains were stopped from running under the river when water tight doors were closed, but enabled an otherwise normal service to resume, key to keeping London running in wartime. We know that Tottenham Court Road Station was one of those used as a shelter at various stages of the war and to assist this a temporary bedding disinfectant storeroom was established in November 1940.

On exiting at street level turn right into Oxford Street and head west. Whilst we do not follow this famous street as far as Oxford Circus, it is worth pausing to consider its experiences during the war. Following the route of the old Roman road *via Trinobantina*, it remains Europe's busiest and most densely populated shopping street with almost 550 stores. Though originally famed for its bear baiting and entertainment facilities, such as the Pantheon, by the nineteenth century retail was the prime business in the area and by the 1940s John Lewis, Selfridges, Marks & Spencer and the now Debenhams (then Marshall & Snellgrove) all had flagship department stores along this road. Selfridges' most famous part in the war effort was to house the cumbersome 80-ton 'Sigsaly' telephone link between London and Washington too large to be located in the cabinet war rooms under Whitehall. Thankfully the equipment survived the V2 rocket that struck and devastated the store in 1945; extensive wartime damage was also suffered by the nearby John Lewis store. On 18 September 1940 an oil bomb fell onto the west house. The fire quickly spread to the east house and the majority of the store was destroyed. The fire raged for thirty-six hours. Firefighter Howard Colenso Gillard, his middle name originating from the Boer War battle his father took part in, lost his life at the incident. The forty-year-old AFS man, along with fellow firefighter Donald Mackenzie, is commemorated on the evocative Fire Fighter's Memorial in the shadow of St Paul's.

The 18 September brought an even greater tragedy to nearby AFS station 72Z located nearby and it is to that site that we now head. Turning right into Rathbone Place and heading north we soon get to the junction with Percy Street. Behind you, occupying numbers 7–9, can be found the original location of Jackson & Allums Garage. These premises were utilized as an appliance room full of London Taxis and trailer pumps with their crews serving the busy W1 area. Nearby, the Westminster Jews Free School in Hanway Place, further crews and a watch room made up one of the busiest AFS stations in the area.

Shortly before midnight on the night of 17/18 September 1940 a bomb struck this three storey garage, whose basement doubled up as an air raid shelter for off duty fire crews and the

Jacksons Garage today leading to the spot where Harry Errington was awarded the George Cross

public living nearby. The initial reports reached Tottenham Court Road Police Station and immediately civil defence crews from surrounding stations were despatched to the scene, including Ambulance station 39, covered later in this walk. On arrival they found that all three storeys had collapsed killing twenty people, including seven firefighters. A fire then broke out in the debris with survivors of the blast becoming trapped. Up top exhausted rescue crews were backed up by doctors from the Middlesex Hospital. Fresh heavy rescue parties sent from Hampstead as they attempted to access any survivors with the help of acetylene cutters, and even the presence of a district surveyor to ensure that the building could be deemed as safe as possible. Nearly five hours into the incident cries of help could still be heard from inside the basement. Police intensified their efforts with rescue squads to remove debris and glass and barricades. Trestles and lighting was also established around the incident.

Beneath the rescue an incredible story of bravery was unfolding. Thirty-year-old Harry Errington, a Soho born master tailor and volunteer AFS man, had been thrown across the basement by the blast. On coming to his senses he found himself surrounded by fire. He was making his way to the emergency exit when he heard cries for help nearby and saw a fellow fireman trapped beneath debris. Instead of going for help and ensuring his own safety Harry turned back. Wrapping himself in a blanket he dug the man out with his bare hands, dragged him up a narrow staircase and out into a small court yard (still present today by passing under the archway in front of you). By now his hands were badly burnt, and being a tailor these were his livelihood, yet knowing this he returned into the blazing building to rescue a second fireman he had seen trapped beneath a radiator. Freeing him he again carried him to the relative safety of the courtyard. All three men were severely burnt but after months of medical treatment returned to the fire service. For this selfless act of courage Harry Errington was awarded the George Cross, the highest award possible and one of only three presented to London fireman in the war.

After the war Harry returned to the family business in Saville Row, eventually retiring as late as 1992. A prime mover in British Basketball, he coached the successful Regent Street Polytechnic Side and was involved in the 1948 Olympic side. Harry finally passed away aged ninety-four in December 2004.

Despite this gallant act the loss of fire fighters Jack Bathie forty-seven, Alfred Abrahart thirty-two, Arthur Batchelor twenty-six, George Bowen thirty-five, Robert George thirty, Benjamin Mansbridge forty-five and Mayer Ward thirty-one in the same incident tore a hole in the heart of station 72Z. The carnage was so terrible that workman carrying out repairs at number 33 Rathbone Place reported the macabre find of a woman's hand from the incident almost a day later.

Leaving this sad spot we continue north towards Charlotte Street. Turning right on Goodge Street cross over Tottenham Court Road into Chenies Street. Stop here and look back at Goodge Street Station. Near to this spot a V2 rocket landed on 25 March 1945 causing extensive blast damage. This had been one of the stations that had been chosen as a Deep Level Shelter started in 1940 and completed in 1942. Although connected to the nearby station, access was often via a separate double spiral staircase with internal lift shafts at each end. A lesson learnt after direct hits at Bank, Balham and Trafalgar Square ended in fatal consequences for people sheltering with only one exit. A large concrete blockhouse at the head of the stairs survives today. Its red and white striped decor looks rather incongruous today given its more conservative surrounding buildings, but when first constructed could hold around 8,000 people in two 1,200 foot tunnels divided into upper and lower floors with iron bunks and lavatories, a problem as they were located deeper than the existing sewage system. Warden's rooms, first aid posts and a state of the art Lamson pneumatic message delivery system, capable of shooting messages around the complex and to the surface, completed this incredible subterranean structure. Each section was named after a famous scientist, including Newton & Faraday, among others. The block we see today formed part of General Eisenhower's London Headquarters from March 1943,

Great Portland Street incident where three firemen lost their lives

The same view today

housing both British and American service personnel. In addition female NFS staff used its space for a hostel and post war it remained in use as army transit accommodation for National Serviceman awaiting passage overseas until, having survived the Blitz, ironically a fire closed the shelter in 1956 for the last time. Before leaving this spot those with an interest in the Great War will be drawn to the nearby drill hall and memorial to the 12th (The Rangers) London Regiment who left from this corner of London to fight at such momentous battles as Gommecourt (Somme), Arras and Passchendaele and, though at great cost, earned a reputation second to none among the fighting men of the Western Front.

Return to Tottenham Court Road, cross over and turning right head north. Before long you come to the American Church in London. This was the original site of Whitefield's Tabernacle constructed in the 1750s. John Wesley once preached here in 1770 when the church was surrounded by fields and gardens. Though the original building was replaced in 1890 by a newer structure named the Whitefield Central Mission, the area was struck on Palm Sunday, 21 March 1945 by the last V2 to strike central London and completely demolished. The church you see

Note the Euston fire stations destroyed turntable ladder appliance that took a direct hit

today was constructed in 1957 and its grounds a public thoroughfare. The 13-ton long range missile arrived at 3,000 miles an hour and the lone Cafe Nero near the mural is all that remains of the pre-war site where thirty-five people lost their lives.

Continue past the church to the junction with Howland Street on your left. Follow this across the next junction into New Cavendish Street and pass the University College Hospital on your right. A number of incidents occurred in New Cavendish Street during the war; incendiary bombs started fires on 20 September 1940, damage was also caused by a falling anti-aircraft shell that fell in the street in the same month having been fired from nearby Regents Park. The worst was to come on 16 April 1941 during a very heavy raid when two HE Bombs landed in the street when many of the properties around you were damaged.

Turn left into Great Portland Street and stop outside No112, on 16 September at 2215hrs the first indications of an incident were reaching the civil defence control rooms. A fire was reported above the air raid shelter at No126. There were already

The name of 'Toby' Tobias on the Fire Fighters Memorial

several casualties being dealt with and fire appliances on the scene when a second bomb landed at 2235hrs, setting alight a nearby gas main. Then a UXB was reported by a shelterer at No126 and the nearby BBC was advised to start evacuating and stop broadcasting while a search for the device was undertaken. This was later found to be a false alarm. The event proved to be a costly one for the men of Euston fire station who had attended. Their District Officer Joseph 'Toby' Tobias was killed whilst directing operations, the second bomb directly hit the stations turntable ladder killing fifty-one- year-old senior fireman Thomas Curson and thirty-one- year-old AFS volunteer Albert Evans outright. Command was taken over by Station Officer Edward Morgan and he was awarded a BEM for his role in this incident. This very gallant fireman had already been awarded a George Medal for rescuing a lady from a blazing building in the great fire raid of 29 December 1940 and would go on to be awarded the King's Police and Fire Service Medal for Gallantry for the rescue of a family from a flat in March 1941.

From outside No112 Great Portland Street, walk south and

All Souls War Memorial

enter Langham Street, which emerges at the pretty All Souls Church in front of the BBC building. The church, designed by Sir John Nash in 1824, has a deliberate circular columned portico to soften the pre-existing corner of Portland Place. On 8 December 1940 a landmine exploded nearby severely damaging the church, which remained closed for 10 years after the war. The impressive Langham Hotel opposite and the BBC Building itself. Adjacent to the church was the site of the Queens Hall, this venue opened in 1893 with a smoking concert attended by Edward Prince of Wales. It was famed for its lavish ornamentation and could accommodate 3,500 people over two floors. It was completely gutted over a series of raids throughout November 1940, and a far more modern building stands on the site today.

Returning to the incident of 8/9 December 1940 on this spot,

The memorial plaque at Queens Hall

an incredible eyewitness account exists that was broadcast later that year. Though the narrator remains anonymous, it provides perhaps the most descriptive account of a parachute mine known in existence;

'On the night of December 8 1940, I left the BBC shortly after 2245hrs and, accompanied by a colleague, Mr Sibbick, went to the cycle shed in Chapel Mews. The customary nightly air raid was in progress, and as we left the cycle shed we could hear the distant sound of aircraft and AA gun fire. We were just entering Hallam Street from

the mews when I heard a shrieking whistling noise like a
large bomb falling. This noise continued for about three
seconds and then abruptly ceased as if in mid air . . . then
came the sound of something clattering down the roof of
a building in the direction of Broadcasting House. I looked
up thinking it might be incendiaries, but this was not so.
We slowly walked round to the entrance of Broadcasting
House . . . I remained outside talking to two policeman;
their names were Vaughan and Clarke. A saloon car was
parked alongside the curb some distance round from the
entrance and I could see the lamp post in the middle of the
road opposite the Langham Hotel. The policeman had
their backs to this so did not observe what followed.

The aftermath of the parachute mine 9 December 1940

Whilst we were conversing I noticed a large, dark, shiny object approach the lamp post and then recede. I concluded that it was a taxi parking. It made no noise. The night was clear, with a few clouds. There was moonlight from a westerly direction, but Portland Place was mainly shadow. All three of us were wearing our steel helmets; my chinstrap was round the back of my head, as I was advised to wear it so shortly after I was issued with the helmet. A few seconds later I saw what seemed to be a very large tarpaulin of a drab or khaki colour fall on the same spot. It fell about the speed of a pocket handkerchief when dropped and made no noise. Repair work was being carried out on Broadcasting House and I, not unnaturally, concluded that it was a tarpaulin which had become detached and had fallen from the building into the roadway . . . I drew the attention of the police officers to it. They turned around and could see nothing . . . Then followed some banter, but I persisted in saying that I had seen something fall into the road. They then decided to go and investigate . . . Vaughan drew ahead of Clarke, who

The Langham Hotel in ruins after the incident

stopped at the curb to ask me exactly where it had dropped. I went over towards him, calling out that I would show him it . . . I went towards the tarpaulin and had reached a spot to the left of Clarke about six feet from the curb, and twenty five to thirty five feet from "the thing", when Vaughan came running towards me at high speed. He shouted something which I did not hear. At that moment there was a very loud swishing noise, as if a plane was diving with engine cut off – or like a gigantic fuse burning, it lasted for about three or four seconds . . .'

He continued the story;

'Vaughan passed me on my left and Clarke, who apparently had understood the shout, also ran towards the building . . . I crouched down in what is known as the prone-falling position number one . . . My head was up and watching and even before I could reach position number two and lie down flat the thing in the road exploded. I had a momentary glimpse of a large ball of, blinding, wild, white light and two concentric rings of colour, the inner one lavender and the outer one violet, as I ducked my head . . . my head was jerked back due to a heavy blow on my steel helmet and I received a further heavy blow to the bridge of my nose and forehead. The blast knocked the helmet off of my head. The explosion made an indescribable noise – something like a colossal growl – which was accompanied by a veritable tornado of air blast. I felt an excruciating pain in my ears and all sounds were replaced by a very loud singing noise . . . I felt that consciousness was slipping from me, and at that point I heard a clear loud voice shouting "don't let yourself go, face up to it, hold on".'

Managing to get himself into a crouching position with hands covering his face and feet against the curb, successive waves of blast continued to pass over him and three further pieces of shrapnel struck him in just a few seconds to the head and chest. Then the debris cloud of dust, dirt and rubble flew past him causing further injuries to his face. The blast of a land mine lasts

The restored view today

for nine seconds and to survive this is quite an incredible occurrence. He was taken to the first aid post at the Middlesex
Hospital. The Commonwealth War Graves Commission lists
PC John Charles Vaughan, twenty-three, from Charing Cross
Road Section House a native of Cardiff as being killed in the
incident; thankfully it appears that PC Clarke did escape. The
Langham Hotel itself was used for military accommodation
during the war and a number of servicemen were killed during
the incident. It was so badly damaged that the BBC took it over
post war as an ancillary building and famously *The Goon Show*
was recorded there. It was in turn re-sold and converted back
into the luxury hotel that stands there today. ·

The damage caused to the BBC Building was so severe that
alternate premises were sought in Bush House. Broadcasting
House, its exterior daubed in camouflage paint, had suffered
previous damage. On 15 October 1940 the seventh floor was
struck by a delayed action 500-pound HE. It fell through the
floors eventually reaching the third floor music library before
coming to rest. Whilst trying to move it from the central core of
the building, just after 2100hrs, it detonated whilst the news
was being read by Bruce Belfrage. The explosion was heard by

listeners tuning in. After a pause the reassuring words, 'it's all right' broke the silence and Belfrage carried on as if nothing had occurred, shaken and covered in plaster and soot, a true professional. Seven of his colleagues died in the blast. The Langham was damaged and a passing bus was destroyed in the blast. The evening's broadcasts carried on throughout this incident. Auntie was doing her bit in wartime.

We now walk north up Portland Place towards Regents Park and take the left-hand junction with New Cavendish Street once again, right into Weymouth Mews and pass the front of the Dover Castle pub. This traditional watering hole was very popular with off-duty civil defence crews during the war, especially the Ambulance crews from Station 39, who feature so heavily in this walk, and it is to their premises that we head now. By turning next left, then left again you effectively come to a peaceful courtyard/garage block at the rear of the pub (there is a back entrance should you require a refreshing drink). This was the location of London Auxiliary Ambulance Station No39.

This busy volunteer station served the West End and many of the incidents covered in this walk. It was one of 130 such

Weymouth Mews home of Auxiliary Ambulance Station 39

The heritage plaque in Weymouth Mews

stations that had almost 10,000 staff tasked with the removal of wounded and often mutilated bodies from the scene of incidents. In the garages at No35/42 were housed the heavy hastily converted ambulances, often ex-commercial vehicles and driven by female ambulance drivers. Later American motor companies saw the benefits of advertising their vehicles 'having survived the London Blitz' and the more modern Detroit-made Ford and Chevrolet vehicles became common sights on the streets of London. The staff were housed at No16 and, as suggested, were mainly female and came from the full spectrum of the nation's social classes and background. The horrors and stresses they had to endure in the war years must have taken an incredible toll on them. As one of the ambulance crews remarked;

> 'No one seemed to think of the trauma involved. It was not impossible to find a rat-gnawed body lying behind a wall.'

Today a heritage plaque marks the spot and an excellent book *The Forgotten Service* by Rosemary Day gives the full story of the premises during the war.

Return via the Dover Castle or by retracing your steps to Weymouth Street, turn left and this in turn brings you to the junction of Harley Street.

This famous street with medical connections was built in the late eighteenth century. By 1860 many doctors had moved their premises here due to the quality housing and close proximity to the major railway stations of Marylebone, Kings Cross, Euston and St Pancras. Florence Nightingale worked in a hospital for 'Gentlewomen' at No1 before leaving for the Crimea, and there are still over 3,000 medical staff employed in the street today. The street does bear the odd scar from the war. Incendiaries specifically took their toll on 13 October 1940 when fires were started at No69, 101 and 121. A High Explosive bomb dropped near to the junction of Weymouth Street on 11 May 1941 and further damage was caused by a falling Anti-Aircraft Shell that struck No33 in March 1943, a month where more Londoners lost their lives to AA Shells than German bombs.

At many of the minor incidents here the rescue services were assisted as ever by the local Home Guard detachment. One of their keenest members carried a pistol and during a raid noticed that somebody in a store had carelessly left two electric lights on despite the blackout regulations. He promptly mounted a stationary London Bus and taking aim, let fly. Within five shots

Harley Street remembers Florence Nightingale

St Marylebone Civil Defence dressed for dinner

the offending lights were extinguished. On the down side, however, considerable damage had been caused to the large plate glass windows.

Often they undertook training operations by night in nearby Regents Park. One was to capture three gates leading onto Prince Albert Road. After a hard night's work these were eventually taken. At the post-exercise debrief it was suggested that with a little more effort, had they been led through the Zoo, they could have captured further entrances, to which the platoon commander replied;

'I had considered that but realized that my name wasn't Daniel!'

Worthy of inclusion in this book is the amusing anecdote told by Charles Graves *The Home Guard of Britain* involving a member of London's Home Guard during the Blitz;

'The Company were assisting in the rescue work and it was noticed by the second in command of the Company that a man was perched very dangerously on a bed of what remained of a second floor. He immediately clambered over the debris, to discover that the man had lost one of his legs and looked in pretty bad condition. With considerable difficulty he managed to carry the injured man

*over the debris to the ambulance, which promptly
conveyed him to hospital. The following evening enquiries
were made at the hospital as to his condition, but no one
appeared to know anything about the incident. The
officer, however, was quite certain that the man had lost a
leg in the Blitz and, what was more, had been sent to this
particular hospital. It was finally established that this was,
up to a point, correct: the injured man was suffering with
slight cuts and shock, and as for the missing leg – he had
lost that in the previous 1914-1918 war.'*

As you reach the northern end of Harley Street you need to
cross over the busy Marylebone Road, and into Brunswick
Place. Turn left into York Terrace and stop outside 43/47 York
Terrace. This is the scene of one of the more bizarre disasters in
the war.

On 11 May 1941 police at Marylebone Lane were alerted to
a serious fire in York Terrace. On arrival a scene of total devastation met the rescuers, as a direct hit of the block you are at
now had occurred. By 0140hrs it had been established that

St Marylebone ARP Wardens dressed for war

numerous people were trapped and up to 100 casualties were in the three buildings that made up this block. The Middlesex Hospital despatched a Mobile First Aid Unit and ambulances sent from Station 39. Moments later from the original incident log we see a hurried note from a warden at post B5 to the fact that a doctor on scene requests at once morphia for sixty casualties, and heavy rescue squad members are requiring club hammers and chisels. This presents an almost voyeuristic glimpse into the immediacy of an event now almost seventy years ago.

It was not until 0930hrs that the bodies had been recovered and persons accounted for. A number of the casualties were in fact members of the civil defence, including Nurse Hilda Field, a sixty-two-year-old holder of the Belgium Elizabeth Medal, a decoration awarded to civilians from the Belgium authorities for valuable service to the military in the Great War. Alongside her were four further female members of the Women's Voluntary Service and Graham Furber, a local member of the Observer Corps. Among the more unusual finds at the site were a large quantity of ammunition and two dead male Pekinese dogs. The exact nature of the building is a particularly strange one as it was the London Headquarters of the Group for Sacrifice & Service, an offshoot of a Californian religious sect of moon worshippers.

Around a hundred of them had gathered to worship the moon under nothing but a glass dome, Dr T Mawby-Cole, a Harrogate businessman and cult member who had predicted that 'something staggering would occur on the 11th May' now lay lifeless alongside fellow worshippers on the porch of the building.

Wardens Eric Wills and James Ireland worked tirelessly alongside rescue chief Andy Sutherland to eventually free up to sixty who were trapped on the ground floor of the building. Many were dressed as priests with rings and brooches donating a hierarchy within the group. The building caretaker, perhaps shaken by events, never the less hampered the rescue operation by insisting that the altar (that needed moving) 'must not be defiled by pagan hands'. It is intriguing that the wardens were withdrawn at dusk and police requested to patrol to prevent looting.

We continue to the junction with York Gate to your right. This is the entrance to Regents Park in which London's famous Zoological Gardens are found. Their story in war is an interesting one and worthy of telling here.

Initially when war broke out the authorities, concerned over large crowds gathering, forced the Zoo to close. Keepers and staff noticed an interesting change in the behaviour of animals that suggested they preferred the gaze of the public; the primates were particularly subdued. Soon it was arranged for soldiers billeted in houses nearby to visit until they were posted overseas. The Zoo did reopen but crowds were drastically down on pre-war numbers. Meanwhile outside of London, parks such as Whipsnade began constructing pens and wire netting to take some of the larger animals who were effectively evacuated for the duration of the air war. Sadly dangerous spiders and snakes were destroyed as the risk of escape was too great in the event of their cases being damaged in a raid. The aquarium was also emptied and dismantled due the amount of glass that presented a danger if broken. Food was initially considered to be an issue if in short supply leading Whipsnade to grow additional food stocks to assist. In reality, however, a constant supply of Blitz damaged foods from the docks, unfit for human consumption, provided more than plentiful. During the bombings the Zoo was hit numerous times with oil bombs and incendiaries, all adding to the considerable damage that was caused. A giraffe died of fright along with some antelopes, and a number of exotic birds managed to make good their escape. Slight damage was caused to the Monkey Hill, Ravens Aviary and Camel House but repaired. The Rodent House and Zebra Pen were totally destroyed, however. On one incident a Grevy's zebra escaped and was chased by staff along the Outer Circle Road towards Camden before eventually being captured. Sir Julian Huxley, secretary of the Zoo at the time and founding member of the WWF, wrote in his autobiography of the event;

'Every time that the AA guns went off the animal bucked violently. I was frankly alarmed that he would kick me in the stomach. When I discussed the incident with the zebra keeper the following day he told me "Cor bless you, Sir. You needn't have been frightened. He's a biter not a kicker!"'

A V1 struck the south bank of the canal in 1944 causing damage to the Owls Aviary and Pheasant House. It is estimated that, by the end of the war, not a pane of glass remained unbroken. The star attraction, Ming the Giant Panda, had also passed away due to natural causes during the war. After peace came the Zoo had just about survived, but had endured a torrid time.

Walk south back out onto the Marylebone Road and turn right to head up to Baker Street. Opposite the junction with Marylebone Road and York Gate you can see St Marylebone Church. This splendid structure took its current shape in 1885 and suffered only minor external damage during the war though all of its windows were blown in. In 1949 the windows were re-glazed but cleverly some original pre-war fragments were incorporated and are visible today. The spot where you stand to the north of the Marylebone Road was struck by a HE Bomb on 15 September 1940, a seminal day in the Battle of Britain but one in which between eighty and 100 raiders penetrated the inner defences of London in two major daylight raids. This was

The St Marylebone Memorial where the York Terrace victims are remembered

The St Marylebone Memorial

at a great cost to the Luftwaffe, however, and whilst it is reported that over 600 aircraft flew sorties over the country in twenty-four hours, 311, just over half, were reported as being destroyed or damaged. The human cost for London was fifty-two killed and 153 injured.

Walk west towards Bakers Street. Before long you reach another of London's most famous attractions, Madam Tussauds Waxwork Museum. Veteran AFS firefighter Jim Morgan once recalled how he fought a large fire here and the staff were evacuating the waxworks of its models and placing them in the street. Under the heat of the incident many began to melt; a bizarre memory as the rich and famous virtually withered away whilst he continued to fight the fire.

As you walk up towards Baker Street station and the walk's end, Roy Perkins, a London Taxi driver during the war, recalls the time he saw an Army bomb disposal unit drive up Marylebone Road with an unexploded bomb on their jeep surrounded by sandbags. Four soldiers were holding onto it whilst the driver sounded the horn. At speed they were rushing to an open space to safely detonate the device. As they reached Marylebone library the bomb exploded, the jeep leapt high into the air and the engine block flew over Woolworths before landing in Harewood Place where the marks in the road surface

A shrapnel scar on a Marylebone lamp post 70 years on

were visible for years afterwards. The scene of carnage was the worst thing that Roy witnessed throughout the whole war.

Continue along Marylebone Road to Bakers Street Station. First opened in 1863 the station suffered bomb damage to its surface structure in 1940 and a strange cylindrical object, later discovered to be a flare container, landed just outside in January 1943. Inside at the top of the escalators, which take you onto the Bakerloo Line, the heavy steel flood doors dating from the period are still visible. When the station was badly damaged in the 11 May 1941 raid one of the London Transport Board Guards described the scene;

'Someone shouted Fire on No4 platform. I rushed out of the room and ran across the rails of No2 and 3 roads and saw flames coming from the inside of a train that was standing on No4 platform. The cushions were alight. When I got near it two men were throwing water on it, so I grabbed two buckets and ran with them to the staff

A risqué cartoon from a Marylebone Warden

lavatory where there was a tap . . . I was looking towards
a fire that was burning on the top stories of Bickenhall
Mansions, when I heard a whistle getting nearer, and one
of the chaps shouted:"Look out! Bombs coming down!" I
and the others turned and ran down the stairs as quick as
we could. I noticed that the others had dropped behind
some ticket machines that were there, but I was slow and
was looking for a place to shelter when the bang came . . .'

He somehow survived the impact and covered in dust with
ears ringing and having sustained numerous small cuts and
bruises, brushed himself down to continue with the many fires
now breaking out in the building.

'As I looked from No2 platform, I saw fires burning in
houses just across from the station, and as they burned
they lit up Bakers Street Station. Whilst standing near the
stationmaster's office I heard five thuds not very far off as
bombs hit the ground, and the ground shook under foot. I
was glad when it became light, but the all clear did not go
until about 6 o'clock . . . when I got to the main booking
hall, what a mess. Glass and woodwork all over the place

and dust, I've never seen such a lot before . . . I never want another night as that.'

In more recent times (1973) two explosive devices were located: one in the ticket hall and one on an overbridge. Both were safely defused without damage or injury being caused, proving London continues to go about its hectic everyday life regardless of the threats or actions of those who seek to derail it. We have now reached the end of our walk.

Published Sources

i – *The Blitz Then & Now* – After the Battle 1988

ii – *The Lost Treasures of London* – William Kent – Phoenix Publishing 1947

iii – *The City That Wouldn't Die* – Richard Collier – Collins 1959

iv – *London Triumphant* – Sidney Jones – Studio 1942

v – *London Taxis at War* – W. Earles – privately published 2006

vi – *London Transport at War* – Charles Graves – LTPB 1947

Chapter Three
The Bermondsey Walk

*Circular walk starting at London Bridge Station and finishing
at Mary Magdalene Church Bermondsey Street
Duration – 3 hours*

Modern day Southwark was created in 1965. It comprises the three old boroughs of Southwark, Camberwell and Bermondsey. The new borough borders the River Thames in the north, with the City of London on the opposite bank, Lewisham to the south and south east, Lambeth to the west, with small boundaries with Croydon and Bromley also on the western side.

Southwark has seen many changes in its recent history; most notably the disappearance of the Surrey Commercial Docks, with its old wharves and warehouses converted to apartments and studios. The old ponds have been largely filled in with a large array of social and commercial housing having sprung up.

The Bermondsey Official Guide of 1937/38 tells us that Bermondsey had a population of 102,700, the street mileage was fifty miles and early closing day was Thursday. (I can just about remember early closing days.)

The Borough arms derived from the parishes of Bermondsey, Rotherhithe and St Olave.

The name Bermondsey derives from Beormond the Saxon Lord of the district, and 'a kind of marshy island when the tide was out and a wide expanse of water when it was in.' Bermondsey is mentioned in the Domesday Book as 'Bermundseye.'

Bermondsey starts at London Bridge and spreads east where it embraces Rotherhithe, which in turn housed Surrey Commercial Docks. The origins of 'Rotherhithe' derive from Redhra 'a mariner' and Hyth 'a haven'.

WALK III - BERMONDSEY'S BLITZ

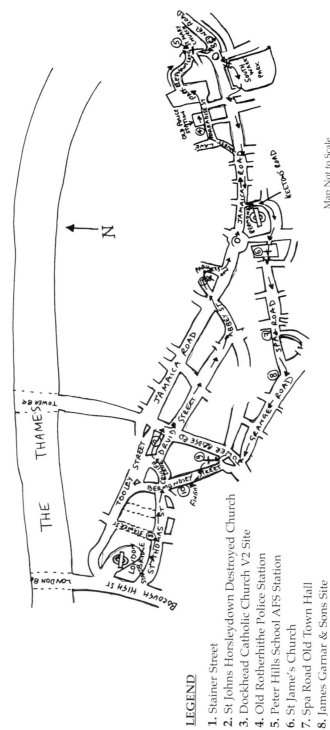

Map Not to Scale

LEGEND

1. Stainer Street
2. St Johns Horsleydown Destroyed Church
3. Dockhead Catholic Church V2 Site
4. Old Rotherhithe Police Station
5. Peter Hills School AFS Station
6. St Jame's Church
7. Spa Road Old Town Hall
8. James Garnar & Sons Site
9. St Mary Magdalene Church
10. Bermondsey Street

The docks apart, the borough was noted for its leather and tanning industry. In the west of the borough, along with food manufacturers such as Lipton's, Crosse and Blackwell and Hartley's. Peak Freans, the biscuit maker, had its factory in an area between Drummond Road and Southwark Park Road, employing 3,500 staff. I can recall travelling up to London by train from Lewisham and you knew when they were making 'Custard Creams' as the smell penetrated the railway carriage. Peak Freans was also targeted by the Luftwaffe as they made prisoner of war parcels.

Prominent churches in the area were St Mary Magdalene at the southern end of Bermondsey Street, St James' in Jamaica Road, again another notable landmark on the railway into London Bridge now sadly being boxed in by developers, the Roman Catholic Church at Dockhead and St Mary's Rotherhithe. Another notable landmark is the Norwegian Church perched on the southern end of the Rotherhithe Tunnel. There are several other Scandinavian churches around Surrey Docks and this is a clue to the type of cargo coming into the docks, namely wood from Scandinavia. There is a lovely granite memorial to the 2,100 Norwegian Merchant Seaman killed in the Great War. The church is worth a visit for those interested in maritime history and I have always been made very welcome on my visits.

Perhaps the crowning glory of the borough in past times was Southwark Park. It was noted for its band season (May to

Pre-war view from Peak Frean's towards Tower Bridge

August). The bandstand has been restored recently by a team of dedicated volunteers. The park was also noted for its winter garden and a fine chrysanthemum show.

The antique market in Bermondsey Square was also renowned throughout the trade. This has sadly diminished into a shadow of its former self, again at the hands of 'progress.'

Next to the market is the site of Bermondsey Abbey. Nothing of the Abbey, whose history spans over 1,000 years, remains above ground.

The Walk

We start our walk on the southern side of London Bridge Station in St Thomas Street. The proximity of the London Bridge area to the City of London meant that the area was always going to be in the front line of the German Luftwaffe attacks particularly in the Night Blitz of September 1940 to May 1941. Two things you cannot camouflage in war are a railway and a river. The railway line into London Bridge runs through south east London and the distinct peninsula of Surrey Docks were both an aid to the German pilots.

The railway line out from London Bridge, during the Night Blitz, was constantly peppered with incendiary bombs and it would be the trains' fireman who would be tasked with clearing these from the track to enable the services to proceed on their perilous journey to suburban areas such as Lewisham, Deptford, Croydon, Dartford and beyond, down to the Kent and Sussex coasts.

On 12 December 1940 a land mine descended by parachute and landed by the signal box of the station. Not going off, naval personnel were summoned to deal with the mine. (Naval personnel would deal with mines as these were naval ordnance.) Perhaps the bravest of the brave were the two signalmen who remained on duty in the signal box during the ordeal. Two Naval personnel arrived and fortunately the mine was made safe. It was conceded that had the mine exploded, the station would have ceased to exist.

Proceed south east along St Thomas Street to the junction of Stainer Street. There is a blue plaque which tells a gruesome story.

Bermondsey Borough was quite a forward thinking council as war approached. Being a large social landlord it felt a duty to protect its citizens and build shelters in the event of air raids. *The Evening News* of 29 September 1939 reported the following;

The Borough of Fortresses – Bermondsey is well dug-in; The Evening News, 29 September 1939

Bermondsey Borough Council officials and workmen have been working like beavers since the war started to complete a comprehensive shelter scheme for the entire population. They have not been content, in this riverside borough, with its factories and densely populated streets, to help only those caught out of doors during a raid.

Mr W.E. Baker, the ARP Controller (his normal job is General Manager to the Council) said to me (writes an Evening Standard rep) "We are providing strong shelters for living in this borough and our scheme will be permanent."

Some are in railway arches – "We had to fight the Southern to get them," said Mr Baker with a smile – "some beneath wharf buildings, on housing estates or any piece of waste ground."

Already there is accommodation on the six-square feet principle, for more than 67,000 people and as a number of

Surface shelter in Stalham Street off Southwark Park Road

shelters are lofty and temporary ones have been erected, all could be given room.

Biggest of the railway arch shelters is London Bridge Station; it has accommodation for 2,000. Altogether nearly 5,500 can be sheltered in arches.

In addition to the Council's own shelters a number of factories hand over their underground shelters as soon as they close for the evening.

Plans had been drawn up for the shelter under the railway as early as 1938. The shelter would house many hundred civilians with the shelter being fortified with five-ton steel doors at each end (Stainer Street and Tooley Street). On 17 February 1941, not a raid of great magnitude, a high explosive bomb pierced the railway at the St Thomas Street exploding and ripping off the steel door, which cascaded along the shelter taking all before it in its wake. Shelters of this size had to have a medical post and the attendant doctor, Lesley Probyn, and her two nurses, Ethel Nixon Little and Rosina Hartley, were amongst the sixty-eight killed; their bodies never being found. A further 175 were injured. To compound matters several hours later a delayed action bomb in a crater in St Thomas Street exploded killing two young Air Raid Wardens, believed to be Charles Heron and John Shepherd, both aged seventeen.

As previously mentioned the arches under the railway were to

Stainer Street Railway Arch Plaque. Until recently that date read 1940. Fortunately it has been corrected

be utilized as shelters but a great deal were used as storage by the businesses in the borough, as well as light industrial workshops. Bevington's, the fur and skin company based in Abbey Street, had their warehouse in 42 St Thomas Street gutted by a shower of incendiary bombs causing a loss of nearly £60,000 of merchandise.

We move along St Thomas Street towards Crucifix Lane, pausing at White's Grounds Estate. During the great raid on the City of 29 December 1940, one Bermondsey Air Raid Warden reported that 'everything that missed the City hit Bermondsey.' One of the delayed action bombs settled in the estate. Sadly the Royal Engineers dealing with it, Captain Crump and Sergeant Bumstead, were killed.

Continue under the railway then cross the road into the church yard of St John Horsleydown. The church was built in 1732 as it took over the parish of St Olave, as the latter was demolished

The bombed out St John Horsleydown, 1946–48

to accommodate the railway. The church was pretty much destroyed by incendiary bombs by October 1940. The shell has been incorporated into the London City Mission. There still remains a rather sad-looking First World War memorial in the shadow of the building in urgent need of restoration.

Come out of the church yard into Tower Bridge Road and turn right. There is a nice plaque on the wall reporting that Sir Thomas Guy, the founder of Guy's Hospital, resided near here. We are not dealing with Guy's in this walk as it was the receiving hospital for Southwark not Bermondsey. St Olave's near Southwark Park on the Lower Road was the Bermondsey equivalent.

Cross over the road to the Cat and Cucumber Cafe and turn left into Druid Street. The St John's Estate here provides us with further evidence of the Blitz. There are several shelter signs on the wall of the estate.

There were three shelters on the estate which could house 135 people at night and 300 hundred during the day. The shelters were located under the blocks.

Molly Fenlon, a resident of the nearby Devon Mansions in Tooley Street, recalled life in the shelters in the area;

'We were an assorted lot there. As I walked up and down I studied the different types of people as they slept. There was a tiny baby, a fortnight old, like a little rosebud in its pram and an elderly man bald headed, snoring fit to wake the seven sleepers spread-eagled on the ground with no blanket between him and the asphalt. I listened and found from ten different types of snore and ten different keys. It was quite interesting! Next morning I discovered that I had collected six flea bites on my person and Miss N was horrified to see a bug crawl across the collar of her raincoat as she was packing up.'

Cross over the road and another blue plaque appears at the junction of Millstream Road. The arch here was being used as a sports and games centre rather than shelter. On 25 October 1940 the arch was hit by a high explosive bomb. Rescue attempts were hampered as a gas main was ablaze at the entrance. The gas would need to be turned off by the Gas Board. It could not be extinguished by water for fear of a spark or further bombs causing a deadly explosion. As a result seventy-seven lost their lives that night.

Carry on to the end of Druid Street and turn left into Abbey Street. We are starting to move into the leather and tanning industry area as Bevington's looms in front of us, now converted into studios and workshops.

However, we continue on to Jamaica Road. Cross over the road and walk over to the Dockhead Catholic Church, a large red-bricked modern church. The original being a worshipping place for the many Irish Catholics who came to England to work in the tanneries, docks and railways. The Convent of Mercy was founded by Catherine McAuley, an Irish nun, in 1839. Many of the sisters went over to the Crimea to tend the wounded in that campaign in the mid 1800s.[i]

We have looked at the Night Blitz of 1940/41, but we move on to 2 March 1945. A V2 long range rocket thundered into Parkers Row, which now runs behind Jamaica Road. The church, the vicarage and convent were wrecked. Four priests and the housekeeper were trapped. One of the first people on the scene was rescue worker, Ted Heming. Ted was a milkman in the early stages of the war, but as the Blitz progressed he became a full time light rescue worker.

The smoke and dust of the explosion at the church was the key for the light rescue team to go into action. Despite the hopeless-looking situation Ted began to burrow into the wreckage. Miraculously Ted heard a voice which he surmised came from

Druid Street Arch plaque

somewhere between the nave and the crypt of the church. Ted had ordered his colleagues away from the scene and began working his way through a v-shaved cavity upside down. He finally located the owner of the voice, Father Arbuthnot, who was conscious, but badly injured. The Father also had his legs trapped by a large beam. It took an almost superhuman effort to free the Father, plus the structure was close to collapse. Also there was a leaking gas main nearby. Fortunately the hole Ted had made getting to the Father was adequate for Ted to pull him through. As they reached surface Ted's colleagues pulled them both out. Ted was overcome with giddiness and passed out. Both were rushed to Guy's Hospital and after treatment Ted was told that Father Arbuthnot had died. However, Ted received a message that the Father had survived. The Father immediately wrote to Ted expressing his deep thanks and the pair became firm friends for life.

The Father was the only survivor from the church.

It was announced in the *London Gazette* on 17 July 1945 that Ted (Albert Edward Heming) had been awarded the George Cross. The citation read;

> 'Although from the outset, it appeared impossible to affect a rescue, Heming refused to abandon the victim and, with great gallantry and determination, successfully accomplished a task seemingly beyond human endurance.'

In 2005 the church held a memorial service to remember the tragedy.

We retrace our steps remaining in the north side of Jamaica Road. We pause briefly at the junction of Abbey Street to think of one of Bermondsey's youngest heroes, Arthur Beecham. His story was told in the *South London Press* of 22 November 1940;

> 'Though suffering from shrapnel wounds, eleven year old Arthur Beecham of Abbey Street, Bermondsey saved his two sisters and his friend from the wreckage of a billiard hall which had been bombed. He then went in search of his mother's friend.
>
> The four children were sheltering under a billiard table when the bomb fell. All the lights went out. Although

Parkers Row after the V2 of 2 March 1945

Arthur's throat, shoulder and stomach were injured, he dug through the debris until he reached his two little sisters, Connie and Doreen aged six and two. Then he set about finding his friend George.

When they were all outside, he found that George's mother was not out. He decided to go and look for her but grown-ups told him that a doorway he would have to go through was about to collapse.

Parkers Row, 1950

22nd Battalion, London Regiment (The Queen's) Drill Hall

He went back getting through the doorway safely. But he was unable to find her. He called to the rescue workers then collapsed. He was taken to Guy's Hospital immediately and it was found that his condition was extremely dangerous and he was likely to die from loss of blood.

But Arthur did not die. He is now in the country with his two sisters. Very soon he will be wearing a presentation watch.'

Also we can see, on the corner of Old Jamaica Road, a modern Territorial Army drill hall. This replaced that of the 22nd Battalion of the London Regiment.

As we continue east along Jamaica Road we can see the effect of the bombing as there was a vast amount of new social housing built in the post-war years. Jamaica Road had a grand array of small shops such as tea and coffee houses, confectioner's grocers, butchers etc. My grandfather Thomas Bright's toilet goods shop was destroyed at number 187.

Continue to West Lane and turn left and cross the road. We are greeted by one of the most ornate war memorials I have seen. It is dedicated to those killed in the First World War from Bermondsey and Rotherhithe and attached is a small plaque to the civilian casualties of World War Two. Over 700 civilians were known to have been killed in the borough during World War Two. It has recently been restored with the aid of the War Memorials Trust

Pass the war memorial and turn right into Paradise Street. Thirty metres along this street on the north side of the road is the old Rotherhithe Police Station, the blue lamp still in evidence. The station cleaner was Joseph Ambrose, a remarkable man. During raids he would go out with the officers of the station to incidents. A series of reports from officers of the station, including the station's Inspector, Cornelius Carson, confirmed Ambrose's bravery. This from PC A. Brown;

> '*On 15 September 1940 at 11.40pm, I was on duty at the front door of Rotherhithe Station when a high explosive bomb fell on the roof of Platform Wharf at the rear of the station. I was detailed to proceed at once to the bombed building where about 1,000 were sheltering. Mr Ambrose, who is always standing by and ready to help, came with me at once. The building was on fire and debris was falling into Cathay Street, along which we had to pass. All the people from the shelter were evacuated safely to other public shelters in the vicinity and Ambrose was conducting parties through the streets despite the fact that bombs were still falling and shrapnel from anti-aircraft batteries in Southwark Park was dropping in the area. The evacuation was completed without a single casualty. On numerous occasions when I have been called out during air raids Mr Ambrose has insisted on accompanying me when he could have remained in the station under cover.*'

This is just one example of how Ambrose helped evacuated damaged property. Another incident involved Ambrose's refusal to stop searching through wreckage where one of the officers, PC Andrews, was buried.

For his bravery Joseph Ambrose was awarded the British Empire Medal.

The building is now private property.

Continue along Paradise Street and straight through the adjoining park to come out in Elephant Lane. Turn right and immediately left into St Marychurch Street until you reach St

Mary's Church and churchyard. There is evidence that there has been a church on this site since the thirteenth century. Christopher Jones, the captain of the Pilgrim ship *Mayflower*, is buried here as is Prince Lee Boo of Pauli, a prince of the Pacific isles.

Behind you is the charming former Peters Hills School building. This building was taken over by the Auxiliary Fire Service to become part of Station 61z of that service.

It is here that we return to the first night of the Night Blitz on 7 September 1940. Following a reprisal raid on Berlin the German campaign on London began in earnest. After the daylight raids London was unprepared for what was to follow. Two hundred and forty-seven Junkers bombers kept up their onslaught until 0430hrs. The attack concentrated on the docks either side of the river; Woolwich Arsenal, Millwall, Limehouse, Beckton Gasworks and West Ham Power Station were the prime targets.

The old Paradise Street Police Station

Peter Hills School Auxiliary Fire Service Station

Surrey Docks had half a million tons of wood stored and twenty-four hours later it was all gone

Surrey Docks can be walked as a separate walk but there is little to see in the context of this walk.

Six fire-boats were recalled back from Thameshaven and one of the officers recalled;

> *'We kept close formation until we reached Woolwich and then we saw an extraordinary spectacle. There was nothing but fire ahead, apparently stretching across the river and burning on both its banks. We seemed to be entering a tunnel of fire; no break in it anywhere. All the usual landmarks were obliterated by walls of flame. Burning barges drifted past. For many hours no contact with the shore was possible. We did what we could where we could as we slowly worked our way up the river.*

At one time we were just getting into position to fight a fire in a large warehouse when the whole of the riverside front collapsed into the water with a mighty splash. The contents of the building, bags of beans, pouring into the river made a sound like a tropical rainstorm. Soon after, we were surprised to see two firemen and three firewomen picking their way along the shore in the direction of Southwark Bridge; they told us they had been cut off in a control room for several hours. They had undoubtedly had a rough time of it, but did not seem unduly perturbed.'

The glow from the firing of wood in Russia Yard, Quebec Yard and Surrey Docks could be seen as far away as Guildford.

Bermondsey is famous for its Boys' Clubs and Mark Say captures the mood in his history of the Oxford and Bermondsey Club;

'The Blitz of late summer 1940 was a sharp shock for a number of Canterbury members of the Oxford and Bermondsey Club. On Saturday afternoon 40 members went down to Hall's Green in glorious weather. The afternoon was spent bathing and watching the battles overhead, little realising that the aeroplanes were on their way to bomb Rotherhithe; that the glows of fire which could be seen over from the camp and the heavy drone of bombers overhead spoilt all enjoyment and Sunday was passed with considerable anxiety. When the boys arrived back on Sunday they found that the club was housing 30 homeless people from Rotherhithe.'

A local lady, Nell Coombs, recounts;

'It started in the afternoon on the dry dockside. And then it sort of went in a circle. They dropped tons of these incendiary bombs. Behind the flats where I live, we were throwing sand on them and we were only kids. Then all of a sudden, evening-ish, as the fire came either side it seemed to cause a whirlwind, all of the curtains of the flats went up because it was August and all the windows were open. All the curtains caught fire because they were blowing out with

this terrific wind. It got worse and worse and worse so we had to evacuate.

Most of us walked. Most people from Redriff walked, all walking along together, all of us getting out, the whole of the area, all roads were made of tarry blocks, so therefore the roads were all alight as well.

There were 844 dwellings down here. I should say there were over a thousand people walking down Rotherhithe Road to get to the Tunnel area, to the main road. They were picked up to go to different schools. And then some parts got blocked, so you couldn't go no more – got set alight – so we were in warehouses. My family was one of the last families to get out. We'd got as far as Amos Estate in Rotherhithe Street. All the people from the nunnery were with us. People volunteered to take us out by car. It was dangerous. I can remember a woman in my car; she was slapped around the face because she was screaming, you know. But earlier on, funny thing, there wasn't any panic. We were all walking along together. We weren't running, we were all walking.'

Surrey Docks, 7 September 1940

The Norwegian Church on the entrance to the Rotherhithe Tunnel

Both roads which led on to the docks, Brunel Road and Redriff Road, were made impassable as the roads buckled from the heat. Naturally the immediate vicinity had taken a pounding. Fire engines from other districts including as far away as Hertfordshire attended only to find that their hoses did not fit the local hydrants. The residents of the peninsula were evacuated in droves against the fiery backdrop.

Retrace your steps on to Brunel Road, cross the road and head back west along Jamaica Road. You can now clearly see the Norwegian Church. Living in a German occupied country, the Norwegians were forbidden to celebrate their Independence Day. Therefore, it was from the church that the BBC broadcasted a service to Norway. As earlier mentioned in this chapter the church is worth a visit.

Cross over the crossings to the entrance of Southwark Park and enter the park. As well as its various attractions the park was also home to an anti-aircraft battery.

Follow the path through the park that runs parallel with Jamaica Road and exit the park, turning left. There is a plaque on the wall of the Millpond Estate which presents a unique souvenir of the Blitz and the two pictures tell the tale.

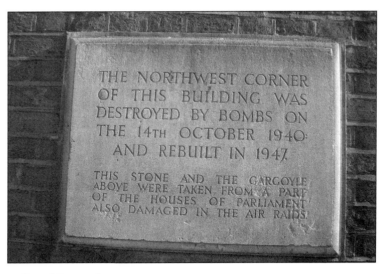

THE NORTHWEST CORNER OF THIS BUILDING WAS DESTROYED BY BOMBS ON THE 14TH OCTOBER 1940 AND REBUILT IN 1947.

THIS STONE AND THE GARGOYLE ABOVE WERE TAKEN FROM A PART OF THE HOUSES OF PARLIAMENT ALSO DAMAGED IN THE AIR RAIDS.

Millpond Estate plaque

Continue west along Jamaica Road, past the modern parade of shops to the corner of Keatons Road, just before Bermondsey Tube Station. A few yards along Keatons Road stood Keatons Road School. It was here the many residents of Surrey Docks headed for as the school was used as a rest centre. Here you could get a drink, some food, maybe a change of clothes; a refuse for those bombed out. However, disaster struck as the school was hit just after midnight resulting in over thirty killed and many injured. Lil Newcombe tells the story;

Millpond Estate gargoyle

'We'd been evacuated to Keaton School and then they
bombed that as well. A lot of them got killed, all from M
Wharf. My dad's face was split open. All the men were
outside, you see, near the shed and most of them got killed.
You just heard this crash, you know, never heard them
coming at all. And you could hear everybody scream. Then
all you was doing was bending over the dead bodies. And
the funeral, when they buried them all, there was nothing
left of them you know.'

The King was so horrified that he visited the scene days after.

The sad irony of this was that Keatons Road was hit during a
raid by German airships in the First World War in 1915. The
date, 7 September!

Continue west over St James' Road into the churchyard. The
church dates to 1829 and is one of the 'Waterloo Churches' as it
was built with money granted by Parliament after that battle. The

Keatons Road School

Keatons Road, 1915

bells of the church were cast from cannons captured at the Battle of Waterloo. A slight amount of shrapnel damage appears high on the wall to right of the main entrance. There is a charming First World War memorial just inside the church to those of the church's Young Men's Bible Class killed in that conflict. The church is often open and is very much worth a visit.

A high explosive bomb hit the lodge of the church on 16 January 1941. The blast damage was so severe that many windows and doors were blown off properties in neighbouring streets. The local Home Guard had to guard these for fear of looting.

Leave the churchyard from the western exit and turn left into Thurland Road and right into Spa Road. Spa Road was the part of the food industry for the borough, housing Lipton's and Pearce and Duff's to name but two. Continue along Spa Road for some way until you reach the old Town Hall complex opposite Spa Gardens. There are three buildings facing you; to the left the Old Library, in the middle a modern block and the Old Town Hall on the junction with Neckinger. The modern block more recently replaced the original Town Hall which was destroyed. The building on the corner with Neckinger took over the mantle of the Town Hall during the Blitz until 1965 and was Bermondsey's Control Centre.

On 15 September 1940 a high explosive bomb penetrated the basement of the original Town Hall in Spa Road killing Muriel Amy Noel, the Commandant of the Women's Legion, and her two assistants.

So, the last great night of the Night Blitz was 10/11 May 1941. Hitler's thoughts were turning to the Soviet Union and resources were needed for this front. But the finale of the Night Blitz was certainly spectacular. As the siren sounded followed by the immediate drone of the bombers one woman commented, 'We knew we were in for a heavy night.' How right she was!

Important buildings across the river were hit including The War Office, Westminster School, The British Museum, The House of Commons chamber was destroyed, the Law Courts, The Public Records Office, St James' Palace and the Tower of London to name a few.

Churches hit included St Stephen Walbrook, St Clement Danes, St Margaret's Westminster and St Mary le Bow.

Fourteen hospitals across the capital were also hit.

Spa Road railway arch shelter, 1939

Spa Road Town Hall
Food Office, 15
September 1940

Albert George Richard Henley was the Mayor of Bermondsey. He was one of the borough's great and much loved figures. A staunch trade unionist, he was tireless in his work for the community during the Blitz. 10/11 May 1941 was just another busy day for Albert. He had been paying money out to the needy from the distress fund, he attended a rehearsal of *Journey's End*, the First World War play at Clubland Youth Club in Walworth. He and wife, Gladys, were guests at a dance at Corbetts Lane Wardens' Post.

Albert returned to the Town Hall, but had gone back there without his lucky jumper.

He and his chauffeur, Eddie Taylor had helped remove a piano off a trapped man, he and his brother, Percy, had put out incendiary bombs in the Spa Road complex. Into the early hours of 11 May he was told that Peak Freans' shelter was hit and was a scene of devastation. Albert lived in Drummond Road and knew many of the factory staff and was on his way to help.

As Albert left the office a high explosive fell with a splinter hitting him. Jack Hart, of the council drivers, was also hit. Albert died in St Olave's Hospital later that day. A sad loss of a great

Albert Henley at tea party for Bermondsey evacuees in Worthing

figure. Henley Drive, on a modern estate just to the south of Spa Gardens, is named in his honour. As a postscript Spa Gardens was formerly housing that had to be demolished after this last great raid.

One distinguished visitor to London and indeed Bermondsey in November 1942 was the Soviet girl sniper Lyudmila Pavlichenko. Fighting near Odessa against the Germans she recorded 187 kills. *The Star* newspaper reported;

> '. . . at Bermondsey she was met by the Mayor, Mr A.C. Starr and she was told that the district had suffered most in the London bombing. She asked how many were killed. The reply was many hundreds.
>
> "Did you ever ask for help outside?" she asked.
>
> "No" was the reply and "I admire your people" was her comment.'

At the end of Spa Road looms the rather grand Alaska Building which was the home of CW Martin's, the fur company. Notably the company made the sheepskin linings for fighter pilots' flying jackets. In early 1940 fire broke out as a quantity of beaver skins caught fire. As well as the regular Fire Service, units from the Auxiliary Fire Service attended, some of the twenty per cent who actually attended a fire before the Blitz.

The basement of CW Martin's was used as a shelter. One night, probably 20 October 1940 a high explosive bomb penetrated K Building, where several hundred were sheltering, travelled through five floors, before shattering on a girder without exploding. On another occasion another bomb destroyed the front office, without any casualties. The blast strew hundreds of tins of food from a neighbouring factory across the local area. The building is now modern apartments.

Barrow Hepburn and Gale had one of their premises in Grange Road. The company was famous for military scabbards and saddles. The Grange Road site received fifteen hits in the Night Blitz, fortunately with no casualties. On 18 September 1940 four hundred people were trapped in the basement as five high explosive bombs struck. The nearby Grange Mills premises had a whole section burnt out as an oil bomb struck with venom. A land mine also relieved the building of every window.

On 30 March 1944 Grange Mills received a visit from General Montgomery in appreciation of the work done.

Barrow Hepburn and Gale, 1941

Grange Mills, May 1941

James Garnar and Sons, the leather manufacturer, had their factory in the Grange between Spa Road and Grange Road. Between September 1940 and May 1941 the company lost eighty per cent of their floor space due to enemy action.

Continue west along Grange Road until you reach Tower Bridge Road. Cross the road to find Trocette Mansions. This was formerly the site of the Trocette Theatre, a highly popular variety entertainment venue for locals. On 11 May 1941 a high explosive bomb landed with full effect.

On the junction of Bermondsey Street and Long Lane stands the Parish Church of St Mary Magdalene. The church has its origins back to the thirteenth century, originally intended as a church for the workers of the Bermondsey Abbey. The current structure dates back to 1830. There is even a 'Watch House' in the grounds which obviously pre-dates the Metropolitan Police. The 'watchman' had powers of arrest and detention for 'disturbers of the King's Peace'.

Fortunately the church did not take too much of a 'buffeting' from the Luftwaffe. The church houses several war memorials, a

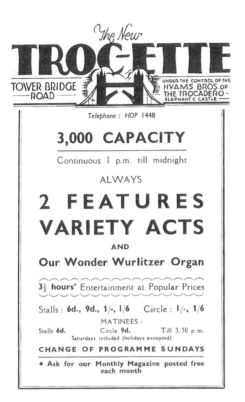

Trocette poster

1944 War Weapons Week plaque, plus a stained glass window to the Royal West Surrey Regiment 'The Queen.'

The memorial service to the victims of the Stainer Street bomb in February 1941 was held here some days later.

Our walk ends here. There are many restaurants in Bermondsey Street and in Tower Bridge including Manze's, the famous pie and eel shop. This does get very crowded at lunch times. London Bridge is a short walk from here and there are buses to the Elephant and Castle and across Tower Bridge.

Chapter Four

The Bloomsbury to Holborn Walk

Start Point – Euston Station (Victoria/Piccadilly/Circle Line)
End Point – Holborn Station (Piccadilly/Central Line)
Duration – 2/3 hours

On exiting Euston Station navigate through the modern office/retail complex and cross the confusing bus lanes to start by the impressive LMS Railway War Memorial. Resplendent with the figures of a soldier, sailor and airman it commemorates men of the railway company that lost their lives in both world wars. On its east face is the inscription that commemorates the men of the railway that lost their lives in the 1939-45 war. In the 1946 publication '*The LMS at War*' the company said of its staff;

'*To all those who faced the crude and stark realities of modern aerial bombardment the strain was unremitting and intense, and be it remembered a far greater effort was needed for them to keep going – as keep going they did – without that rigid training in discipline such as the services undergo before battle. The courage of the railwayman became proverbial. They worked until they dropped on the track and in their tracks. They were wounded, scalded, burned, and yet carried on. They flirted with death on countless occasions to save property, passengers and the lives of their own comrades. A number were killed outright at their posts. For at the back of everyone's mind was that primary duty of the railways – the service which knows no stay, no stop – to keep the lines open and the traffic moving.*'

WALK IV - THE BLOOMSBURY TO HOLBORN WALK

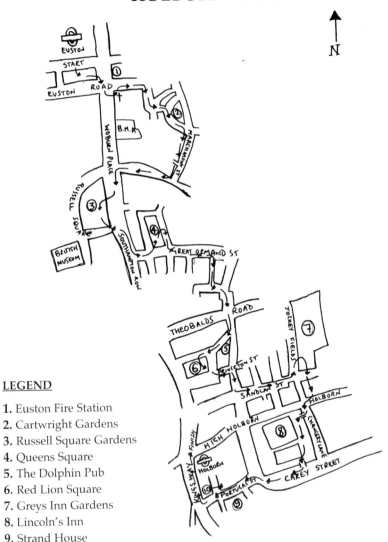

LEGEND

1. Euston Fire Station
2. Cartwright Gardens
3. Russell Square Gardens
4. Queens Square
5. The Dolphin Pub
6. Red Lion Square
7. Greys Inn Gardens
8. Lincoln's Inn
9. Strand House
10. The Old Curiosity Shop

Map Not to Scale

LMS Fire-watcher looking out near Euston

The LMS War memorial
Euston Square

Many of the railway staff enlisted in the armed forces and in theatres across the globe. Some, however, stayed a little closer to home and enlisted in the 37th County of London (LMS Euston) Home Guard. This close knit unit had the additional pressure of guarding long stretches of railway line from attack in addition to their buildings. During one raid Sgt H. Whittock was severely wounded when blown ninety feet by a blasting bomb. He recovered his senses sufficiently to free an officer who had been trapped in the wreckage of a building destroyed by a bomb. For his gallantry he was awarded the George Medal. On a separate occasion the unit's quarter master C. White climbed into a railway wagon that had caught fire. He threw out the burning contents and saved the spread of fire thus, saving the threatened buildings around him. Both he and Sgt J. Holland, who extinguished twenty incendiary bombs in quick succession during the heavy raid of 11 May 1941, were awarded certificates of gallantry for their efforts.

From Euston Square Gardens we get a good view back over the modern station, constructed in the early 1960s and described as 'one of the biggest acts of Post War architectural vandalism in Britain'. Of the original structure only the two Portland stone entrance lodges and the war memorial remain as a teasing glimpse of its more grandeur past. To be fair to the designers the original building had suffered a degree of damage during the war. During the 11 March 1941 raid, Arrivals Foreman at the station, Ted Streeter, was on duty when nearby St Pancras was hit;

'Hold on they're coming in the station . . . They were indeed, and 15,000 panes of glass were coming with them, when they picked themselves up from the archway they'd dived into, there was a ringing in their ears that lasted for weeks . . . the soot from the shattered Victorian roof inside the main station was like black whirling snow, a crater with the lights of the Metropolitan Railway winking 100 feet below and ten ton concrete slabs piled 300 yards away. The debris spattered on the roof of Euston Station, half a mile away, Ted Streeter couldn't believe his ears either. He told his mates "I think it's raining" . . .'

Further damage to the station was caused on 19 October 1940 when incendiaries set fire to the roof of the now demolished

Station 74 Euston Fire Station

Great Hall, and HE Bombs made a crater between platform No2 and 3. The station roof was also damaged as were offices in Drummond Street and the west wing of the Euston Hotel.

On the corner of Euston Square and the Euston Road can be seen a very impressive fire station; the building dates from 1902 and was Station No73 of the London Fire Brigade. State of the art when built, it consists of four floors of accommodation and two appliance bays. During the war years the Regional Fire Officer Sir Aylmer Firebrace, who became Chief of the Fire Staff, National Fire Service on its creation in August 1941, also had his offices here.

Whilst the station itself suffered only minor damage there were a number of close misses, particularly a parachute mine that exploded on the Euston Road on the night of 16/17 April 1941, a raid known as 'the Wednesday'. Crews at the station served St Pancras, Marylebone and Somers Town, all three of which were heavily bombed, they unfortunately lost a number of personnel on duty. Toby Tobias, Thomas Curson and Albert Evans are all mentioned in the Marylebone walk but Frank Hurd died of injuries received on the 29 December at West Smithfield. When the BMA Building in Upper Woburn Place was hit by a parachute mine further lives were lost, more of which later.

The Place, the old Artist Rifles Drill Hall

Crossing over the busy Euston Road we arrive at St Pancras Parish Church, sometimes referred to as the 'New Church'. It dates from the nineteenth century and served the people of well-to-do Bloomsbury when first opened. Through both wars its crypt was utilized and its walls must have shook when the parachute mines in Tavistock Square and Euston Road exploded close by. A combination of blast damage and dry rot forced its closure for renovation in the early fifties. Note the removed church railings as part of the salvage effort outside the entrance. Return to Euston Road and walk east until you reach the junction with Dukes Road. Turn right.

Ahead of you is found a red stone building known today as 'The Place', an arts centre for the local community for the last forty years it was once the drill hall for the 28th (Artists Rifles) London Regiment throughout both wars. The street ahead of you is a Dickensian treasure of architecture. It appears to have survived the bombings intact and often provides modern film-makers with a ready-made historic backdrop. Follow it around to the left and then right into Burton Street.

The large brick building is the rear of the British Medical Association, designed by Sir Edwin Lutyens. It was badly damaged on the night of 17 April 1941 when a land mine detonated in Tavistock Square outside the front of the building. A fire was already raging nearby and in the consequent blast firefighters Harry Skinner and Stanley Randolph were both killed. Their colleague, Arthur Preece, died of his wounds on 29 July in Berkhamsted Hospital from the same incident. All three men were from the nearby Euston Station No73 and were in Costain House at the time the mine went off. The BMA is no stranger to tragedy. In more recent times both the IRA and latterly the 7/7 bombers have left their mark on the property.

We continue to the left-hand turn into Burton Place that joins Cartwright Gardens. At the rear of the building on the corner of both can be seen the effect of bomb damage on the building.

Cartwright Gardens is a pleasant Grade II listed semi circle of Georgian mansions, built in 1810 for the City Guild of Skinners. In the small park are a couple of tennis courts. The original park suffered extensive bomb damage during the war. The railings have been replaced but the ever present London trees are particularly impressive and could tell a tale or two. I was once told by a park keeper that reinforced chainsaw blades are used when cropping these ancient trees throughout the parks of London due to the danger of embedded shrapnel that remains within them. Today most of the mansions are hotels with student

Damage at the rear of Cartwright Gardens

accommodation on the far side of the square; we head south to the fashionable shopping Marchmont Street.

An eclectic mixture of architecture is the first clue to the damage caused here. Between No 27/37 the modern Post Office replaces a number of Georgian properties such as a boot makers and drapers that had lain derelict since hit by a bomb on the night of 16 September 1940. A number of original features still predate the war, however. The Marquis Cornwallis pub was damaged but is today a splendid spot for liquid refreshment. Note also the parish boundary markers dating back to 1791 that mark the borders of Bloomsbury and St Pancras. The best description of this street in warfare is found in Basil Woon's *Hell Came to London* published in 1941;

> '*Take Marchmont Street in Bloomsbury where I do my shopping for example. I don't suppose the censor will mind (considering the time which must unfortunately elapse before this book can be published) if I state what every London knows; that Bloomsbury has been hard hit . . . Yet in Marchmont Street, thoroughfare of humble retailers, not a shop has closed, except, indeed, those which have been hit, or evacuated as dangerous by the police. The butchers, the greengrocers, the bakers, the creameries, the delicatessens, the tobacconists, the newsagents, the restaurants and the arty tea shops which are symptomatic of Bloomsbury's student population, are all open and doing business as usual.*
>
> *The shopkeepers themselves are all at their accustomed places by eight o'clock in the morning. I notice a few fresh faces among the assistants, but that is because many have been called up. There has been no evacuation and no panic, and what is true of Marchmont Street is true of every other district in London.*'

At the bottom of Marchmont Street, turn right towards Russell Square on Bernard Street and cross the junction with Herbrand Street. Ambulance Station B, for Bloomsbury, was located at No19 Herbrand Street with its satellite auxiliary Station 56A located nearby at No 3/16 Woburn Place.

Pass the entrance to Russell Square Station, used as a shelter during the war. Constance Holt, the wartime editor of *Woman's Own*, described the scene;

> '*Most of the tube stations were taken over as shelters, as there weren't enough big public shelters that people could get to. Russell Square Station was one of these. I remember on several occasions coming back from the theatre by tube, and when I got out at Russell Square they had put bunks all along the platform, and you'd see women putting on their face-cream, doing up their curlers and getting right for the night. Of course you'd politely not stare at them because they were in their bedrooms. I remember there was a little bit of snobbery about stations. I heard one woman say, "Oh, us and our family go to Regent's Park now, it's nicer people". And the children used to go for rides on the tube. At least their mothers knew where they were, and it was much safer than the street.*'

As well as doubling up as a shelter, the station was a very important part of London's wartime defences being one of those fitted with huge floodgates that could be closed during air raids. We emerge out onto Southampton Row and see Russell Square. The most impressive hotel overlooking the square is the Hotel Russell, designed by Charles Fitzroy Doll. It suffered fairly heavy damage in the war, notably the stunning mosaic flooring that was struck in late 1940.

Another hotel, the Imperial, was damaged on the fire bomb raid of 29 December 1940 and Constable Francis Taylor of the wartime reserve lost his life here trying to usher the public to safety.

To the south west corner of Russell Square on Montague Street can be found the world famous British Museum. Some of its smaller items had been safely stored underground in the Aldwych tunnels when war came. However, the building itself was badly damaged. One incident that occurred on 11 May 1941 involved the museum's director Sir John Forsdyke;

> '*The incendiaries ploughed through the copper roof of the British Museum, burning fiercely in the high timbered rafters between roof and plaster ceiling. As the first fire*

engines came racing across the courtyard, the museum's director, Sir John Forsdyke, went pelting to meet them, the doughty little Greek scholar taking a header onto the running board. It took only twenty minutes to realize the position was hopeless. Not only the rafters were burning but the Roman Britain room . . . the Prehistoric Room . . . the Greek Bronze Room . . . empty now of art treasures but an integral part of the threatened building. On the roof choking black smoke drove Sir John and the fireman back. Suddenly with a roar the flames wrapped around the south west quadrant book stack, climbing like a beacon to the sky. Sir John and a fireman struggled across with a jet but after a minute they gave up, "we might as well be spitting on it".'

Thankfully no one lost their life in the incident but the buildings shows the scars of the raid today at its entrance and goes unnoticed to the large queues of visitors waiting to enter.

The nearby disused underground British Museum lies beneath the Nationwide Building Society. It was closed in the mid-1930s

British Museum Underground Station preparing as a shelter 1940

The plaque on the Bedford Hotel

but is, to all intents, still intact beneath the surface. With platforms and booking hall, it is reputed to be haunted. It was, however, briefly re-opened as an air raid shelter on 8 September 1940 and used throughout the war.

Our route now takes us south along Southampton Row, and follows air raids from the Great War often overshadowed by the events of 1940/41. Stop outside the entrance to the modern looking Bedford Hotel. A small plaque on the wall commemorates the Gotha Bomber raid on this area on 24 September 1917. A 110-pound bomb was dropped on this spot killing thirteen people and injuring a further twenty-six. The Gotha Bomber brought a new terror to London when the raids started in June 1917. They continued until the May of the following year before heavy losses to aircraft and crews, along with a changing tide on the Western Front, brought about their end. A huge monster of an aircraft, it had a crew of three and a range of over 500 miles, with a length of over forty foot and a wingspan of almost eighty

The point where a Zeppelin shell landed in Queens Square

foot. It became a foreboding clue to the next air war to come in 1940. Crossing Southampton Row we enter the tranquil Cosmo Place that in turn brings us into Queens Square. Enter the tidy Square from the southern end and walk to the north east. A keen eye will spot a small Great War bombing memorial set in brickwork. It marks the spot where a Zeppelin bomb dropped and exploded on the night of 8 September 1915 and celebrates the fact that even though a thousand people slept in nearby rooms overlooking the square, not a soul was hurt.

From this spot we can also see the statue of Queen Charlotte. For many years this was misidentified by locals and historians alike as being that of Queen Anne. Overlooking the statue in 1940 was a young lady called Joan Weller. She had previously been bombed out of Islington and Twickenham and with her mother was re-housed here as her mother took a job as building caretaker. Joan told an intriguing story of an incident that occurred during the period of April/May 1941. She recalled;

'During a raid we would all go to the shelter in the basement, including Mother, the only exception being an elderly foreign lady too frail to descend the stairs and happy to take her chances up top. This was frowned on but allowed

through some of the earlier raids but in mid May we had a
particularly heavy one (likely to be 11 May 1941) . . . *the*
sound of bombs exploding in the area was far worse than
anything we had experienced so a gentleman decided to go
and assist the lady into her shelter. He disappeared and on
returning alone, summoned my mother to listen for herself.
My mother went to investigate and before too long both
returned looking shaken and speaking in hushed whispers.
Well my older brother worked for the intelligence section
at the air ministry at the time and the following day, after
a phone call from mother, he arrived in a car and escorted
the lady away. We never saw her again. Sometime later,
after the war, Mother told me that they had heard Morse
code being sent from inside the lady's bedroom and that she
had been a German.'

I have never been able to verify the story entirely but Joan, who
was in her nineties when she first told me it, was adamant it was
in this very square you now stand.

One of the buildings in the square, the National Deposit
Friendly Society, a shelter for local residents, was struck on 16
October 1940. Though the raiding on this day was on a smaller
scale than in previous weeks forty-six Londoners lost their lives
that evening, eleven when this building was hit, among them
seven-year-old Leonard Dagger who died along with his older
brother Albert in the incident.

This area of Bloomsbury houses many hospitals. The one that
lines the east side is the Royal Homoeopathic Hospital. This was
used to treat casualties during the blitz, a number of whom died
here. Eighteen-year-old Robert Burns was working at the
Wenlock Brewery when it was hit on 9 September 1940 and
passed away here from his injuries five days later.

We leave Queens Square via Great Ormond Street; the world
famous Children's Hospital is found here and was itself bombed
on a number of occasions and was particularly damaged on
25 November 1940, Basil Woon expresses his anger at this in
1941;

'buildings, shops, cinemas, factories, blocks of flats,
boarding-houses, hotels and humble homes – are down all

over the place. You cannot walk a hundred yards in any direction without seeing some sign of damage. Hardest hit, as usual, have been the hospitals, with which Bloomsbury is filled and which presumably make the place of a 'military objective' to Hitler.

I don't know the proportion of buildings that has been hit, but I think one in ten has suffered some sort of damage. Every night for a week a hail of bombs of all calibres has fallen in the neighbourhood, and every evening, after the all too brief and becoming briefer daylight respite, residents prepare themselves for more. No one really expects, when he emerges from his shelter in the morning, to find his flat, or his house, or his workshop intact.'

Walking along Great Ormond Street we note that AFS Station 66Z was located in the technical school for women complex with an annex at No35. G. Bailey and Sons' sign writing still adorns the wall at this spot. The station consisted of a watch room, appliance room, sleeping accommodation and a mess room and its crews would have dealt with the majority of incidents described in this area.

We turn into Orde Hall Street and head south. The buildings on the left are pre-war and show minor scars on the wall. The area to the right, however, houses completely new, post-war buildings and shows us the scale of damage that occurred in this area, mainly from out of control fires caused from incendiaries. In a rather more matter of fact description, Air Raid Warden Barbara Nixon worked in this sector and wrote of an incendiary raid in her 1943 book *Raiders Overhead;*

'Our first incendiaries gave us a lively night, but as they only descended in dozens, not in thousands, we managed them very easily. The public and most wardens persisted in calling these showers Molatov Breadbaskets, in spite of articles and diagrams in the press, which showed that the whole point of the breadbasket was considerable poundage of high explosives contained in the same case as a number of small incendiaries. The ones we received were scattered from simple tin containers, their dangerous quality lay in their numbers. We were standing in the doorway of our

*sector post when our first shelter descended with a rattle
and clutter. An HE comes down with purpose and direction, but incendiaries sound more like an accident with a
tray full of tin cans, and it is difficult to believe that they
can be responsible for such a holocaust as they created later.
Most of them fell in the road, and we ran about with zest,
dumping sandbags on them. One or two fell in houses and
needed stirrup pumps and I got landed with the pumping,
one has to learn of these things. Jackie had one all to himself
and one landed on to a Miss Heywood's bed on the top
floor of No8 and she had dumped two buckets of earth and
three of water on it and said it was all right now . . .'*

At the end of the road is Dombey Street. The damage to the
top floor of No10 is obvious to this day. Turn left and then right
into Lambs Conduit Street. At Long Yard in this street an
eighteen-year-old Ratan Kavarana was killed on the 15 October
when the premises were struck. Turn right and head to the

Damage at Dombey Street

junction with Theobalds Road. This busy road is the route of the wartime No38 bus and provides the setting for an interesting insight to the early days of the bombing, as described by warden Barbara Nixon;

'*All through Sunday and Monday the East Enders drifted miserably westwards, looking for shelters. Most of them had no baggage; they had lost everything. Some carried pathetic and clumsy bundles of their remaining belongings, some pushed battered perambulators stacked with salvaged, broken treasures. They had nowhere to rest, nowhere to wash. In the West End attempts were even made to exclude them from some shelters. On a No38 Bus a wretched looking women with two children got in and sat down next to me. They still had blast dust in their hair and their tattered clothing, they were utterly miserable, and the lady opposite moved her seat and said loudly, that people like that should not be allowed on buses. Fortunately, the conductor announced with promptitude that some ladies could get taxis.*'

Cross over Theobalds Road and pause on the south side. The street was subjected to many nights' raiding. On 11 May 1941 an AFS Leading fireman, Morrie Zwaig, was trying to extinguish a fire near this junction;

'*I was petrified by the throb of the planes . . . the savage pummelling of the guns . . . the nerve tangling scream of bombs . . .*'

Things were about to get worse for Morrie who was fighting a conflagration in Theobalds Road. The water suddenly stopped as the mains in Red Lion Street was hit by a bomb. In haste he smashed a manhole cover and started pumping water from the sewer system. The filthy job was compounded by the filters clogging up and could only be cleared by hand.

Further along the street a man kept nipping in and out of a blazing shop and began to pile up sewing machines on the pavement. Sometime later he reappeared with a wheel barrow and, having loaded up, trudged off. It was never ascertained whether he was the shop proprietor or an opportunist by the onlooking and overwhelmed fire crews.

We shall head into Red Lion Street, pausing at the junction with the Dolphin Pub. These premises were struck in the Great War on the night of 9 September 1917. It was hit by a high

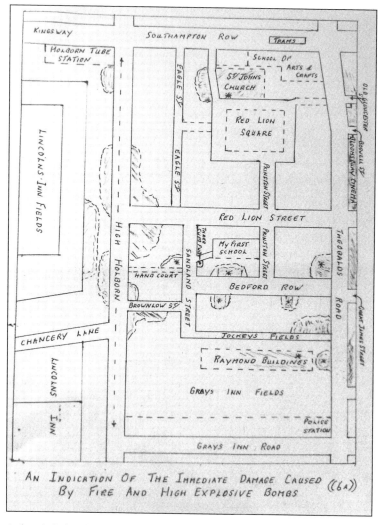

A detailed sketch map of bomb damage in Red Lion Square and surrounding streets

explosive bomb dropped from Kapitan Leutnant Mathy in Zeppelin L13. Three men were killed, one of them, Fireman Green, died of burns while trying to put fires out in nearby houses. Mathy features elsewhere in this book on our Greenwich walk. Inside the pub the clock supposedly stopped at the exact time the bomb struck, 1752hrs, though it is suggested this changes from time to time. We will head right into Lambs Conduit Passage. On the right-hand side the gap between No14/15 gives clues to a since forgotten incident. At the end of this cut-through we emerge into Red Lion Square and Conway Hall, home since 1926 of the South Place Ethical Society. A delightful period-building it appears to have survived the war intact.

Some parts of Red Lion Square did not fare so well and at the west end of the square occurred one of the biggest disasters to occur in Holborn.

The crypt of St John's Church had long been used as a shelter by local residents and wardens alike during heavy raids. They had yet to witness a night like 17 April 1941, however, and Holborn appeared to be singled out for special treatment. In total 658 Luftwaffe aircraft flew sorties over London between 2050 and 0518hrs, many crews flying multiple missions. 890 tons of HE and 151,230 incendiary bombs were dropped during this period. Late on in the evening the church took a direct hit. Many people were trapped in the debris for hours whilst the local rescue services were trying to free them with the raid still in progress. Local hospitals were put on standby to receive casualties from the area. When the rubble was finally removed dozens had lost their lives. Three members of the Clark family, Herbert seventy, Olive fifty-three and Cynthia twenty-two died in the blast. Herbert & Olive lived in Brighton and were visiting their daughter who lived and worked in the city. The church was never rebuilt after the war. Leaving this sad place we leave the square via Princeton Street and turn right into Red Lion Street. An incident in Princeton Street is recalled by Warden Barbara Nixon;

'One knew that the cockney was seldom happy for long, away from London, but one had not realized how extraordinarily devoted he was, not only to London but to his borough area and his actual street. I tried to persuade an old lady of over eighty to apply to the evacuation office. She

had been bombed out utterly and completely, and had no possessions except the clothes she had been wearing. She lived by herself and like many others believed that her 10 shillings a week pension could only be paid to her local post office and if she left she would have to literally starve or live on charity. She simply said "but miss, I couldn't leave London". On discovering that she had a daughter and two sons living in a north London borough that was a relatively safe area I suggested she stay with them but . . . "oh no, I couldn't live anywhere else but Princeton Street, miss" . . . but Princeton street was flat and would not be rebuilt for years and I left her searching for a room just around the corner so she would be on the spot when rebuilding started . . .'

After a short stroll down Red Lion Street turn left at the Old Nick pub into Sandland Street and walk to end of the road where you find an entrance to Jockey's Fields that adjoins Gray's Inn. Robert Menzie visited this area in 1941 and describes the scene;

'8 March 1941 one hour to spare, so walkabout for Fresh air. Holborn, Grays Inn Road, Theobolds Road, Red Lion Square, Lincolns Inn Fields – looking lovely in a cold blue grey mist with a touch of sunlight. Every here and there A FEW HOUSES DESTROYED; A SHOP BLEWN UP. We talk of spirit – (each of everybody else's spirit!), but what tragedies of lost or ruined lives must be behind these shattered bricks.

It is a bedlamite world and the hardest thing in it is to discuss and decide (as we do in The War Cabinet) policies which, even if successful, must bring the Angel of Death into many homes. In public affairs at this time the successful leader is he who ignores the individual and thinks and acts in broad terms.'

Enter Gray's Inn. This is one of the four Inns of Court established here since 1370. During the Second World War, the Inn was badly damaged during the Blitz in 1941, with the Hall, the Chapel, the Library and many other buildings hit and almost destroyed. The rebuilding of much of the Inn took until 1960.

Raymond's Buildings were especially badly damaged as the sketch map shown displays. There were numerous incidents in and around the pleasant courtyards you now walk. Trainee barrister Irene Berti was killed on the 25 November 1944 at 11 Gray's Inn Place when a V1 struck the grounds just after 1100hrs. There was further loss of life in earlier raids where fifty-eight-year-old Charlotte Marsh of 13 Gray's Inn Residences was killed on 27 September 1940 and on 17 April 1941 fire-watcher Frederick White was killed nearby.

Topographical draughtsman, historian, lover of London and part-time fire-watcher Sydney R. Jones saw his city destroyed around him. A Great War veteran, he feverously scoured his favourite spots of the capital in an attempt to sketch and describe them before they were lost forever. The result was his fine work *"London Triumphant"* published in 1942. Of Gray's Inn he writes;

'Grays Inn, I always found, possessed peculiar delights. Being situated beyond Holborn, and a good way from Fleet

Damage visible in Gray's Inn today

Gray's Inn in 1941

Street, it seemed to be very self contained and sequestered. The characteristic blocks of seventeenth and eighteenth century buildings were especially good, and no Inn could show anything finer than Gray's Inn Square.'

Few of the original buildings described by Sydney survived the war and we leave via Fulwood Place out onto High Holborn. Looking left we see the 1914/18 war memorial in the distance. This whole area was one huge conflagration on 11 May 1941 as firefighters and rescue squads fought to prevent the entire area being lost to fire. Earlier on the 9 September 1940, heavy day and night raids had struck central London. In one incident on this street nine Civil Defence workers were killed when the building they were in, Lincoln House, was hit. Among them Auxiliary Ambulance volunteers Dorothy Brooks (Driver), Sylvia Cox and Violet Cruikshanks were all killed when their vehicle was hit. Sgt Joe Snelling of the Home Guard and Edward Bushell of the London Heavy Rescue Service were killed in the same incident. The building is today restored as an office block. We are going

High Holborn in April 1941

to cross Holborn and walk south down Chancery Lane towards Lincoln's Inn Fields.

Alongside No76A is a narrow gateway, open weekdays between 0700/2000hrs. Enter Lincolns Inn here (if out of hours an entrance can be found further down on the right). As you emerge into a pleasant courtyard via an arched entrance shrapnel scars are almost immediately visible. This forecourt houses the home of the Inns of Court Regiment on your left-hand side. This famous territorial army regiment had its HQ damaged in a raid on the evening of 18 December 1917. The scars are obvious on both sides of the buildings. A small plaque commemorating the event is to the right of the entrance to the building; less obvious is the circular stone disc in the road surface marking the actual spot where the bomb struck.

In this courtyard there was an AFS fire station annexe building housing a watch room, mess room and sleeping accommodation located at No7.

Leaving Stone Buildings, as this area is called, we continue south into Old Square. More damage is visible and a small plaque

Holborn after the bombing

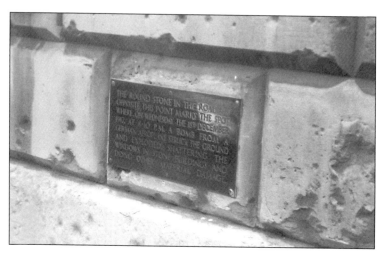

The Inns of Court HQ Great War air raid damage

Lincoln's Inn was badly bombed in both wars

on the building in front of you records the fact that on the evening of 13 October 1915 a Zeppelin dropped a bomb on this spot, shattering the chapel windows and damaging the buildings. A similar stone marker can be found in the roadway marking the impact of the bomb.

Continue south once more and we come to an open area where the war memorial is situated. Pause here and take in the plush surroundings. Lincolns Inn was damaged on numerous occasions in the Blitz. Sydney Jones records his feelings towards this spot;

'For me Lincoln's Inn had personal associations. Years ago, when I returned from the Great War in France, it sheltered my body and ministered to what was left of my soul. For that I will be ever grateful. After experiences on the Somme, Passchendaele, the 5th Army retreat to Villers Brettonneux, and the final glorious advance over the Hindenburg Line, the change from war's alarms to the calm seclusion of Lincolns Inn meant a great deal.'

Things were not always as peaceful as Sydney would suggest. When the area was struck by a bomb on 9 September 1940, Alfred Abbott, himself a Military Medal winner from the Great

The old WH Smith HQ Portugal Street

War was killed near this spot. Constable Charles Squires, a thirty-nine-year-old member of the Police War Reserve from nearby 154 High Holborn, also a Great War veteran, was killed here during a raid on 16 October 1940. When the nearby Royal College of Surgeons was hit on 11 May 1941 William Sansom described;

> *'The Royal College of Surgeons building in Lincoln's Inn was hit, and at this incident rescue workers were given the strange task of rescuing parts of pickled bodies.'*

Post Warden Victor Wooten corroborates this story in his memoirs;

> *'I heard rescue workers report a heavy casualty list, then realised they were saving specimens in pickle!.'*

The building was badly damaged by bombing, however, and among the lost specimens were the plaster cast hand of Patrick Cotter, the Irish Giant, the skeleton of the elephant 'Chunne' and the macabre mummy of the wife of Dr Van Butchell. Elegantly attired and deposited here by her husband since 1775 for over 165 years she had remained unburied before a Luftwaffe cremation did the job in 1941.

We walk past the herb garden and exit Lincolns Inn via the highly decorative grey and white stone archway to emerge into Carey Street. Turn right here passing the back of the Royal Courts of Justice, badly damaged in April 1941. AFS Fire Station 62Z operated out of the building on the right-hand side of this road with an appliance garage and sleeping accommodation.

Our next and penultimate stop can be found by turning right into Searle Street and left into Portugal Street. Follow this until you reach Strand House, the building on your left that was once the headquarters of WH Smiths. During the Great War this was an important building as it housed the Postal Censors Office for all mail to and from the Western Front.

A delightful pair of plaques can be found, one of which shows actual wartime damage. The company had their own part to play in the war effort. Often credited with being the first chain store in the world, its railway station outlets kept commuting

Londoners updated with the latest war news. London Transport put information kiosks alongside these stores, providing travellers with up to the minute news of disruptions in their journey due to bombings and in Parliament Square the Westminster Home Guard utilized a hollow statue base as a blockhouse and disguised it as a WH Smiths news-stand. In 1941 they established mobile news-stands to replace bombed out shops and it is estimated that more than 5,000 staff of the company enlisted in either the armed forces or civil defences during the war.

From this spot it is a short walk out onto Kingsway passing the Old Curiosity Shop in Portsmouth Street. Its frontage was blown out in 1940, though it still claims to be the inspiration for the Dickens book of the same name. Many Dickensian students distance themselves from this as it was not a shop at all when the book was written in 1840, a century before it was bombed out.

We have now reached the end of our walk and on entering the busy Kingsway look right and Holborn Tube Station can be seen in the distance.

Published Sources

I – *The Lost Treasures of London* – William Kent – Phoenix 1947

II – *The City that Wouldn't Die* – R Collier – Collins 1959

III – *Carry on London* – R Calder EUP 1941

IV – *London Triumphant* – Studio Press 1942

V – *Raiders Overhead* – Barbara Nixon – Lindsey Drummond 1942

VI – *Westminster at War* – William Sansom – OUP 1947

VII – *The Blitz* – Constantine Fitzgibbon – Allan Wingate 1957

VIII – *Hell Came to London* – Basil Woon – Collins 1943

Chapter Five
The Old Southwark Walk

The name 'Southwark' is deemed to derive from the 'Suthring-agewoerc', a name which suggests military work. The name was first recorded in the tenth century.

The borough was created in 1900 and stretched across to Waterloo in the west and bordered Bermondsey on the eastern side. It encompassed the Elephant and Castle and stretched along the Walworth Road where it meets the old borough of Camberwell.

Southwark had its own zoological gardens between 1832 and 1862 just off the Walworth Road and another attraction is still this day the Cuming Museum which was described as 'a British Museum in miniature'.

The Borough Market, sandwiched between the railway to Waterloo East and Southwark Street, dates back to the thirteenth century. It is famous for its fruit and vegetables, though now-adays grander fare is on offer.

Possibly the most famous resident was a young Charles Dickens who lived with his father in Lant Street, off of Borough High Street. His father was imprisoned in the King's Bench Prison for debt.

Southwark was home to a variety of industries. Waygood Otis, the lift company, had premises in the borough as did Spicer's the paper manufacturers. Courage's Brewery was a feature in the borough until recent times. Many Fleet Street newspapers house their motor fleets in the borough due to the proximity of the newspaper industry.

Hats and caps were made in great quantity with Southwark being the home of the bowler hat. In the 1850s an order came to Locke's of St James' from the Coke family of the Holkham Hall Estate in Norfolk for a close fitting hat for the estate's

WALK V - THE OLD BOROUGH OF SOUTHWARK

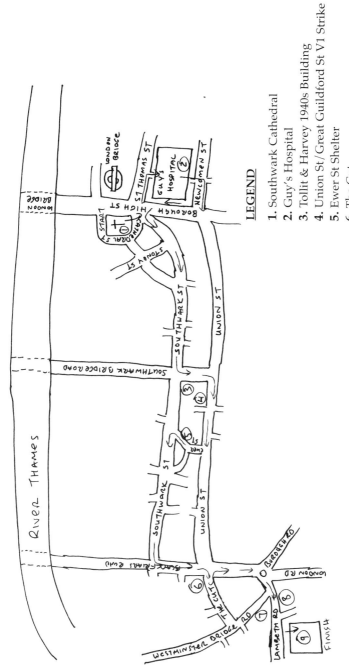

LEGEND

1. Southwark Cathedral
2. Guy's Hospital
3. Tollit & Harvey 1940s Building
4. Union St/Great Guildford St V1 Strike
5. Ewer St Shelter
6. The Cut
7. Morley College
8. St George's Cathedral
9. The Imperial War Museum

Map Not to Scale

gamekeepers, which wouldn't be knocked off whilst they were riding through the woods. The order was passed down to Victor Jay's of Southwark Bridge Road and the design was given to their designer Thomas Bowler. The term 'bowler' became synonymous with that design over the next thirty years.

Wright's Coal Tar Soap, Galloway's Cough Syrup, and Oxo are names all with roots in the borough and Perrier Mineral Water had premises at Bankside. Sainsbury's head office was in Stamford Street for many years.

The population of the borough in 1936 was just over 150,000, greatly reduced in modern times.

The Walk

Our walk starts at Southwark Cathedral and finishes in Geraldine Mary Harmsworth Park, the home of the Imperial War Museum. (2 ½ hours.)

Mention the word 'Southwark' and one immediately thinks on the cathedral that nestles between the Thames and the railway.

The Cathedral is also known as The Cathedral and Collegiate Church of St Saviour and St Mary Overie, and although it has only been a cathedral since 1905, the majority of the present structure dates from between 1220 and 1420, making it the first Gothic church in London. In 1897, the nave was rebuilt under the direction of the architect Sir Arthur Blomfield.

There has been a church on this site since at least 1086 when the site is mentioned in the Domesday Book. The present day cathedral authorities claim that a convent was founded on this site in 606 but this is harder to prove. It was designated a cathedral in 1905 when the Church of England created the Diocese of Southwark.

The cathedral survived the Second World War largely intact but in common with many similar buildings, the main casualties were the stained glass windows, the majority of which were destroyed or damaged. Four windows in the North Transept escaped damage and the large West Window was only slightly damaged. A window commemorating Dr Wood, a local physician, was removed for safe keeping, as was the old glass in the Harvard Chapel.

Unfortunately, many of the best known windows commemorating Chaucer, Shakespeare, Alleyn, Massinger, Beaumont, Fletcher, Bunyan, Sacheverell, Johnson, Goldsmith and Cruden were all destroyed on 11 May 1941 when a high explosive bomb fell in nearby Borough Market, which also destroyed part of the churchyard wall and sadly killed six people in the Market.

On 26 September 1940, a UXB was found in the grounds of the cathedral. This later exploded leaving a crater three-feet wide by six-feet deep but causing no major damage to the cathedral.

It seems likely that the shrapnel damage on the walls of the cathedral was caused most probably by the incident on 11 May 1941, as the shrapnel marks are on the walls of the cathedral immediately adjacent to Borough Market.

We leave cathedral grounds and move through Borough Market. We can pause to remember the night of 29 September 1940 when Wardens' post five at the Borough Market Mission Hall, Great Guildford Street. *The Daily Telegraph* report of this loss reads as follows;

'Nine ARP Wardens were killed yesterday when a heavy bomb fell direct on their underground post in South London. They were buried under tons of bricks and masonry.

All were dead when they were reached by rescue squads which had worked in relays for hours. The victims included a father and two sons and another pair of brothers.

Among the relatives standing by was a bus conductor in uniform. His two brothers were lying under the wreckage. His remaining brother was in hospital, injured three weeks ago by a bomb which killed three other relatives.

The dead Wardens were; Harry Cheeseman, who worked at Woolwich Arsenal; Victor Cheeseman, his son, a turner; Albert Cheeseman, his other son, a brewery worker and chief of the post; Fred Darvell, a butcher, Tom Darvell, his brother, a caretaker; Isaiah Fewtrell, a tile fitter; AS Clark, a pastry cook; Edward Shanks and Jack Holt, a messenger.

The only survivor of the 10 Wardens when the post was struck, Sydney Taylor was blown out of the entrance passage by the blast.

Victor Cheeseman was married three weeks ago; his wife has evacuated to Devonshire. Clark, who was 35, signed on

Memorial plaque Southwark Town Hall

for his first shift as a paid Warden eight hours before the post was struck.

*The Darvell brothers, who were both borough councillors, had completed their tour of the sector and had signed off when the bomb fell.'

Southwark had eighteen Wardens' posts. In comparison neighbouring Camberwell had nearly seventy. Wardens' Grove in the borough remembers these men, but is a small dingy epitaph and, I feel, a scant memory.

The control centre for Southwark was in the Town Hall which was located in Walworth Road and hosts the memorial in the photograph.

We leave the market and move on to Borough High Street. Cross the road, head right and turn into St Thomas Street. Cross the road and proceed to Guy's Hospital. Enter main courtyard. We are greeted with a statue of Thomas Guy (1644?-1724), the founder and patron of this world famous teaching hospital. Guy was known as a bookseller and publisher and also made his

---

* It was in fact the Cheeseman brothers who were councillors as opposed to the Darvells.

Nelson Burgess (in the light coat), Air Raid Warden at Guy's Hospital with colleague, Jack Howard (LMA)

wealth through wise investment in Government stock. The hospital was founded in 1721.

Guy's was the receiving hospital for the borough of Southwark and on five nights during the Night Blitz had over 100 people in casualty. The hospital was largely evacuated during the war. The hospital was hit by enemy bombs over seventy times during the war. Guy's had its own Wardens, headed by Chief Warden, Nelson Burgess. He kept a fascinating Wardens' log which is available in the London Metropolitan Archives.

The first of the high explosives fell on 15 September 1940 and many followed. On 29 December 1940, the great raid on the City of London, Guy's was in the forefront. Nelson Burgess declared that the whole of the commercial centre around the London Bridge had been destroyed.

One of the Guy's nurses recalled that night in a letter to a family member;

'We have had a terrible time and were all evacuated in the middle of the night on Sunday. The whole of Guy's was surrounded by fire and at one time we could not have got out. There was not enough water. What we had stored was soon exhausted and the Thames was at its lowest. As it rose *water was procured and a way made for ambulances. The patients were taken first, then nurses and staff and finally sisters leaving only the men who were our air raid wardens, the acting matron and the acting superintendant (both bosses being away). It was ghastly but again, thank God no-one was hurt . . .*

'*Not one casualty in the whole hospital. Downs Brothers, the huge instrument shop at the Gate was burnt out. The whole of Newcomen Street behind Nuffield House burnt out. (The flames were licking our walls and breaking our windows.) We had fires on our balcony roofs and on the Nurses' Home roof. The Jesus College is half burnt down and a petrol station on the other side of the hospital was blazing. A bomb hit the road outside the massage building and burst through the floor of a ward.*'

The hospital received structural damage and the repairs are evident on the buildings around the forecourt. Incidentally the statue of the founder was boarded up during the war.

Guy's Hospital repaired damage

Guy's Hospital and surrounding area in 1943

Guy's staff were quickly on the scene after the Stainer Street Arch incident recalled in the Bermondsey walk.

Move through the arch directly opposite the entrance to the courtyard. There is a small war memorial to hospital staff killed in the Boer War and also a relic of the old London Bridge.

We now enter the beautiful memorial garden which houses an arch with the names of Guy's staff who fell on service in World War One and World War Two. It is worth recounting that Guy's medical staff were sent out to the concentration camps after the war to treat the victims once the horrors of the camps were discovered.

We leave Guy's via the exit to the left of the arch on to Newcomen Street and turn right and proceed to Borough High Street. If we turn left we come to Borough Tube Station. One of the old tunnels in the station was converted into one of the safest air raid shelters in the country. It could house literally 12,000 seventy feet underground.

Brandon House on the corner of Marshalsea Road and Borough was the site of Moser's Iron Merchants. On 22 January 1945 a V2 Long Range Rocket struck killing thirty-five and injuring nearly 300.

However, turn right on to Borough High Street; almost directly opposite is Union Street. We will return to Union Street later in the walk. The two following photos reveal a remarkable then and now perspective. Pre-war No84 was a wire manufacturer, No86 William Smith's Dining Rooms and No88 was Woolloton and Son's Hop Merchants.

Borough High Street was famous for its coaching inns, numbering over twenty in its pomp. The most famous and indeed a noted tourist spot is the George Inn. A landlord was almost a political figure and a prominent local citizen. Often it was a shrewd move to change the name of an inn, if it was the 'King's Head,' to the 'Queen's Head' or vice versa if a monarch of a different gender came to the throne.

Smith and Co had their premises in the High Street and one of their employees produced this detailed bomb map.

Cross the road and head north. We reach one of the most striking World War One war memorials in the capital and over the left shoulder on the wall of the 'Slug and Lettuce' is a memorial to the men of the Hop Exchange who were also killed in that conflict.

86 Borough High Street during the Blitz

86 Borough High Street today

We turn left into Stoney Street where we see another then and now shot of the Borough Market. The 'then' showing damage from May 1941.

Turn left into Southwark Street and we are greeted on the opposite side of the road by the magnificent Hop Exchange building; now small offices and studios. Built in 1837 it provided a perfect trading centre for the flouring hop trade in the area which by the 1930s housed thirty flourishing hop houses.[i]

The picture shows the Hop Exchange in 1944 and closer inspection shows a barrage balloon above. Fortunately the building was fairly untouched during the Blitz.

Continue along Southwark Street until we reach the junction of Southwark Bridge Road. At numbers 44 and 46 Southwark Bridge Road were manufacturing stationers, Tollit and Harvey

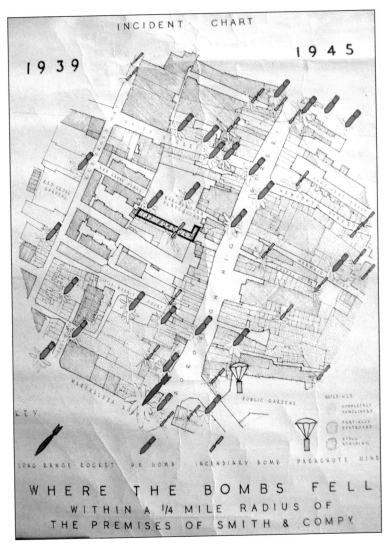

Smith & Co bomb plot map

Ltd. Their Wardens' diary describes how local firms in the area were hit, such as Barclay and Fry, Johnson Riddle and Wilcox's. During the raid of 29 December 1940 Tollit and Harvey had their counting house and machine rooms blasted. The anony-

The corner of Borough Market and Southwark Street, May 1941

mous author also reported that Southwark Street towards Blackfriars Road was hit particularly badly.

Cross over to the west side of the road and turn left. We can see evidence of the blackout imposed on the country from 1939. During the 'Phoney War', from September 1939 to summer 1940, more civilians were killed in traffic accidents due to the restrictions on lighting and lights on cars. One solution was painting white markings on places of potential danger such as on the kerb of sharp turns and bollards. We are presented with some bollards with their blackout paint still apparent.

Turn right into Union Street and pause at the junction with Great Suffolk Street.

The Hop Exchange, 1944

Blackout bollards
in Southwark
Bridge Road

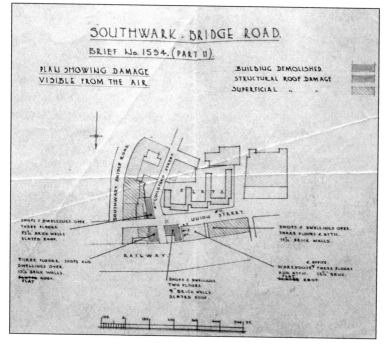

Union Street flying bomb incident map, 19 June 1944, TNA

On 19 June 1944 a V1 flying bomb thundered into this junction and as seen in the map of the incident 'X marks the spot'. Note that the map is 'upside down' geographically.

Forty-nine people were killed here this day with many more injured. Premises on the north side of the Union Street were obliterated, as suggested in the map, including light industrial units and retail business. The estate on the south side of the road only went up in the 1930s and the scars of war are evident in the rebuild.

Sainsbury's Cold Stores, in the vicinity had already been struck by a high explosive bomb on 10 September 1940 with a large fire ensuing.

Continue west along Union Street. There are more bollards in Pepper Street, but continue west and turn right in to Ewer Street, a small insignificant cut back through to Southwark Street. However, Ewer Street housed a public shelter. On the night of

Damage to Union Street from the 19 June 1944 flying bomb

10 September 1940 a high explosive bomb scored a direct hit on the shelter with devastating effect. The incident log for the borough reported 'many casualties, some trapped under the wreckage'. Twenty-one bodies had been pulled from the wreckage after many days of searching by rescue parties. These were mostly residents of Union Street.

At the end of Ewer Street, turn right into Lavington Street; again the camera affords us one of those then and now moments.

Turn left into Southwark Street and cross over to the north side. Earlier we touched on how Southwark Street was badly hit on 29 December 1940. Wright's Coal Tar Soap was set on fire as was the Southern Railway property in Hopton Street. Also Charles Letts, the famous diary company, was ablaze in Southwark Bridge Road. Another casualty was Victor Jay's, our esteemed hat maker.

Perhaps the three following photographs capture the scene.

Lavington Street/Southwark Street

The first pictures the premises of Allardyce and Co Ltd along with the Selecta Gramophone Ltd. The next photograph is in 1941 after the ruined building had been demolished and the third a modern day shot.

89 Southwark Street, 29 December 1940

89 Southwark Street, 1941

We continue west and come to the junction with Hopton Street. It was in Hopton Street that the first female Air Raid Warden was killed. Elizabeth Jane Kerwin was on her patrol when a high explosive bomb hit Nelson House. The Peacock

89 Southwark Street today

Public House was also damaged with casualties there too. Mrs Kerwin's feet were blown off in the blast. She was rushed to hospital but did not survive long.

The area was also subject to a German air raid on 13 June 1917. The raid was carried out by Gotha planes of the 3rd Bombengeschwader.

A high explosive bomb landed on the premises of the British and Bennington (Blue Cross) Tea Company at 118 Southwark Street. The ground floor and strongroom were demolished. Three were killed and five injured in the strong room. A teacher from a large local school, possibly in Roupel Street, described the mood as she rushed back to her classroom from her meeting when the warning was sounded. 'I found fifty little girls aged between nine and eleven under the direction of a nine-year-old, kneeling as instructed in the air raid precautions against the wall farthest from the window.'

Southwark was badly hit on the raid which was the 'Luftwaffe's birthday gift to Hitler' on 17/18 April 1941. Hitler's birthday being 20 April. There were many casualties as a high explosive bomb hit the vicinity of the railway bridge over Southwark Street and Blackfriars Goods Yard.

We leave Southwark Street to learn more of this raid and turn

Paved cross behind Christ Church, Blackfriars Road

Christ Church, Blackfriars Road burnt out

left into Blackfriars Road, cross the road and walk south to the modern Christ Church. We move to the rear of the church to find a paved cross in the grass. On that night of 17/18 April 1941 the church was set on fire from incendiary bombs as were many buildings in the area. The parishioners watched woefully as their church burned. The wooden cross fell from its mount on the spire, landed bold upright on fire where it stood for ten seconds or so before falling on the grass. The *Daily Mirror* likened the scene to 'a fiery cross summoning Highland clans to battle.' The cross was removed to leave a charred image in the grass. Southwark Council duly paved the area where the cross lay as a permanent memorial to the incident. A church had been on this spot since 1670. The new church was completed in 1960.

We leave the churchyard and head back into Blackfriars Road

and turn right towards the railway bridge. We pause under the railway bridge to look at the shrapnel damage on the white tiling of the bridge. This was probably caused by a raid on 25 October 1940. The area was badly hit this night. A high explosive bomb hit the railway viaduct with the Wardens' log reporting fifty casualties. One tram was destroyed and three others severely damaged. It was common practise for trams and buses to shelter under bridges during raids. Also hit was the Ring Boxing Hall on the northern side of the junction with Union Street to such a degree that it had to be demolished. It had formerly been the Surrey Chapel before following a different path. The Palestra Building now sits on this spot. Palestra being Greek for 'a place where wrestling takes place'. The Ring was also a wrestling venue.

One former resident of Nelson Square recalled that day and described his brother's journey to work;

'Going to his office one morning, Horace reached a railway bridge crossing the Blackfriars Road. There had been an air

The Ring, October 1940

Blackfriars Road 25 October 1940

*raid, and the tram cars which had been travelling in both
directions along the middle of the road had taken shelter
under the bridge. There were six trams – three on each of
the tracks (three facing in one direction and three in the
other). A bomb had fallen onto the railway bridge and so
onto the trams beneath it. Horace, like many other passers-
by, boarded one of the trams to help the people trapped
inside; he picked up a teenage girl to take her outside and
her head fell off.'*

Turn right into The Cut and proceed to the Young Vic Theatre
on the junction of Greek Street. The small plaque tells its own
story as Walkin's bakery took a direct hit from a high explosive
bomb. The scene must have been one of utter devastation as the
countless bodies were pulled out of the demolished bakery.

We head back to Blackfriars Road and walk towards St
George's Circus. Blackfriars Road and area was hit many times.
The road leads from the City to one of the most important road
junctions in the south of England during the war, the Elephant
and Castle. The A2 starts at 'the Elephant' as do roads west.
Roads lead to routes over London Bridge, Tower Bridge,
Southwark Bridge and Westminster Bridge. The railway

provided an important link north-south of the Thames. All of these factors providing links in the war effort. Hence deliberate targeting of the area by the Luftwaffe.

The same night as the railway viaduct was hit a high explosive bomb hit the junction of Boundary Row killing two people. On 17 September 1940 the junction with Webber Street was hit with several casualties.

As we near St Georges Circus, there is a modern student accommodation building, McClaren House. On the wall is a plaque dedicated to seventeen Fire Service personnel killed on the last night of the Night Blitz, 10/11 May 1941.

The modern building was originally the Surrey Theatre, but had been unoccupied since the mid-1930s. With water often a problem when fighting the fires of the Blitz, Emergency Water Supply (EWS) tanks were created, often in the basements of bombed out buildings. On this night the seventeen firemen on the plaque went into the basement of the old theatre to connect their hoses to the tank. A high explosive bomb thundered the building,

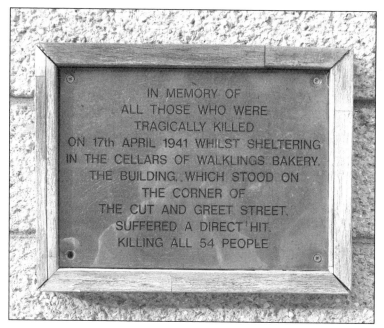

Walklin's Bakery plaque

killing them all as they prepared to tackle the fires around the Elephant and Castle. These men were mostly from Mitcham and Lee Green Fire Stations. There are many of these plaques around our capital with more to follow thanks to the great work of Stephanie Maltman and her team.

We turn right into Southwark Bridge Road and on the junction with King Edward Walk on the opposite side of the road is Morley College which has its roots back to the late 1800s. Its mandate was to 'raise the moral and material standards' around Waterloo Road. It has become a noted adult education college offering a large range of courses.

The college is just in the borough of Lambeth, but we must remember a twin tragedy which hit this borough on 15 October 1940. The college was used as a rest centre, until a high explosive bomb struck and demolished the building. Dozens were killed with many injuries. Bodies were being pulled out weeks later.

On the same night people were sheltering in the shelter trenches in nearby Kennington Park when a high explosive bomb

Firemen's plaque, Blackfriars Road

Morley College, 15 October 1940

did its deadly work. It is estimated that over one hundred were killed, but only around fifty were in a condition to be identified. The Friends of Kennington Park campaigned for a memorial to be erected in the park, which was duly unveiled on 14 October 2006.

Face left and proceed along St George's Road and on the left is St George's Roman Catholic Cathedral. The cathedral was opened in 1848, the first Catholic cathedral built since the Reformation. It was the work of the architect, Pugin. By the end of the Night Blitz the cathedral was all but destroyed. The rebuilding of the cathedral was completed in 1958. The Catholic Girls' school, Notre Dame, across the junction was well ablaze on 10/11 May 1941 like a great deal of the area.

This is a good place to complete the walk with the Imperial War Museum beckoning a visit. The museum itself was formerly the Bethlem Royal Hospital, which is now located in Beckenham in Kent. The museum was founded in 1917 and opened to the public in 1920. It is located in Geraldine Mary Harmsworth Park

St George's Cathedral, 1958

which was often the scene for Home Guard parades.

Refreshments are available in the Park, with bars and cafes towards Lambeth North Tube Station. The Elephant and Castle is in easy reach, as is Waterloo.

Home Guard in Geraldine Mary Harmsworth Park

Conclusion

Many famous and some not so famous eyewitnesses of the incredible, terrible period in London's long history have contributed their experiences to this book, one however provides a fitting conclusion on the Blitz. Constantine Fitzgibbon, wrote the following words in 1957 summing up his feelings on the bombing campaign;

'They looked the fear straight in the face and decided that the reality, horrible though it was, was neither so bad as the expectation had been, nor so repulsive as the alternative of surrender to a wicked and cruel enemy must be. Civilian morale did not crack then; and there is no reason, despite hysterical publicists and strontium-mongers, to assume that it would crack again, even if the conditions were far, far worse.

That is one lesson that may be learned from the Blitz. Another is the extraordinary adaptability, of the inhabitants of a great city. Some people have talked, in the past, as though the bombing of London were a battle fought between the Londoners, particularly the civil defence services, and the Luftwaffe. This is not quite true. A fight in which one man stands defenceless while another punches him is scarcely a fight at all. But what is true is that the people of London displayed enormous ingenuity in dodging the punches as best they could, and enormous resilience in their ability to recover and to accept more punishment. Thus, though they in no sense "defeated" the Luftwaffe, they frustrated Hitler's purpose, and that was a very real victory.'

Night Attacks on London, Numbers of High-Explosive Bombs to the Hundred Acres on some of the most Heavily-bombed Boroughs

Note – The following list is based on British records of the numbers of bombs (irrespective of weight) dropped on London boroughs from the night of 7 October 1940 to 5 May 1941, and includes only those boroughs which reported a total of more than fifteen bombs to the hundred acres. For obvious reasons it gives only a rough indication of the relative density of the attacks as between one borough and another.

Borough	Number of HE per 100 acres
Holborn	39.75
City of London	29.53
Westminster	28.85
Shoreditch	23.56
Southwark	23.25
Stepney	20.02
Finsbury	19.11
Chelsea	18.51
Bethnal Green	17.26
Bermondsey	17.16
Lambeth	17.14
Deptford	15.73

*Source
Official History of the Second World War – The Defence of the United Kingdom Basil Collier – HMSO 1957

Appendix II

Boroughs or Districts in the London Civil Defence Region Reporting over fifty Flying-Bomb 'Incidents'

Borough or District	Number of 'incidents'
Croydon	140
Wandsworth	126
Lewisham	117
Camberwell	82
Woolwich	82
Greenwich	73
Beckenham	71
Lambeth	69
Orpington	67
Coulsdon & Purley	58
West Ham	57

Notes

1 'Incidents' include those caused by bombs brought down by the defences

2 In general each 'incident' was caused by one bomb

3 The total number of reported 'incidents' in the LCD Region was 2420

* Official History of the Second World War – The Defence of the United Kingdom Basil Collier – HMSO 1957

Appendix III

Civilian Casualties caused in the United Kingdom by Bombing and by various Forms of Long-Range Bombardment

	Killed	Seriously Injured	Total
Bombing	51,509	61,423	112,932
Flying Bombs	6,184	17,981	24,165
Rockets	2,754	6,523	9,277
Cross Channel Guns	148	255	403
Totals	60,595	86,182	146,777

Of these 146,777 casualties, 80,397 (including about nine-tenths of those caused by flying bombs and roughly the same proportion of those caused by rockets) occurred in the London Civil Defence Region, and 66,380 elsewhere. Casualties to service personnel are not included.

*Source
Official History of the Second World War – The Defence of the United Kingdom Basil Collier – HMSO 1957

Appendix IV

Locations of Ambulance Stations in Boroughs covered by this book As of February 1944

GENERAL SECTIONS

Western – Allen Mansions, Allen Street W8, 12 Phillimore Terrace, W8

North Western – Lawn Road, Hampstead NW3, 22 Lawn Road, NW3

Eastern – Brooksby's Walk, Homerton E9

Brook Section – Shooters Hill Road SE18

South Eastern – New Cross Road, SE14

South Western – Landor Road SW9

ACCIDENT SECTION

(B) Bloomsbury – 19 Herbrand Street, Tavistock Place WC1

(O) Westminster – 93 Regency Street SW1

(P) Old Kent Road – 301 Idleton Road, SE15

Headquarters – 3/5 Lambeth Road, SE1

AUXILIARY STATIONS

(39) – 35/42 Weymouth Mews W1 (Vehicles), 16 Weymouth Mews (Staff)

(41) – 28/29 Bruton Place W1

(42) – Adelphi, Savoy Place WC2

(56A) – Russell Court, 3/16 Woburn Place, WC1

(58) – 6/9 Upper St Martin's Lane WC2

(115) – Ancona Road LCC School, SE18

(117) – 43 Kings Highway, SE18 – Southend Crescent SE9

(118) – 58 Eltham High Street, SE9

(126) Christ's College, St Germans Place, SE3

(139) – Tower Bridge LCC School, Faor Street, SE1
(141) – Peter Hills School, Rupack Street, SE16
(148) – 179/191 Borough High Street, SE1, Chapel Court, Borough High Street SE1
(TS1) – Trafalgar Garage, Park Row SE10 (Vehicles) Flats 4/5 Trafalgar Tavern (Staff)

Source – LCC Records and the National Archives

Locations of Selected Fire Stations
Covered by this Book 1939/1941

Northern Division HQ Southwark

A District
A3 Westminster

B District
73 Euston
66 Clerkenwell
72 Soho

C District
A34 Shadwell
A35 Millwall

D District
44 Shooters Hill
52 Lee Green
40 New Cross
43 Greenwich
54 East Greenwich

F District
1 (HQ) Lambeth
60 Southwark
61 Dockhead
82 Old Kent Road

AUXILIARY SUB STATIONS

2Z – Marylebone Grammar School, 248 Marylebone Road NW1 (annexe Central Garage, Harewood Avenue, NW1)

11V – Lords Cricket Ground, St Johns Road, NW8

5V – University Motors, 11 Down Street, Piccadilly

73 – (HQ) 173 Euston Road NW1

73W – Christchurch School, Herbrand Street WC1 (annexe Daimler Hire Co, Herbrand Street WC1)

73X – Clipstone Street School, New Cavendish Street, W1 (later 18 Upper Woburn Place)

73Y – Maple and Co Ltd, Tottenham Court Road, W1

74Y – Princess Road School, NW1 (annexe Curators Lodge, Zoological Gardens NW1)

62U – Bank Chambers, 329 High Holborn, WC1

62Z – Royal College of Surgeons, Lincolns Inn Fields, WC2

66Z – The Technical School for Women, Queens Square WC1 (annexe G Bailey & Sons, Great Ormond Street WC1)

72Z – Jacksons Garage 7/9 Rathbone Place, W1 (later 5/11 Mortimer Street W1)

44X – Brook Hospital, Shooters Hill Road, SE18

43U – Randall Place School, SE10

43X – Rangers House, Chesterfield Walk, SE10

54W – Charlton Manor School, Nigeria Road SE7

54X – Invicta Road School, SE3

1U – Holy Trinity School, Carlisle Lane SE1

1V – Beaufoy Institute – Black Prince Road SE1

1Y – Surrey CCC, Kennington Oval, SE11

60U – John Harvard School, Copperfield Road SE1

60V – Friar Street School, Webber Street SE1

60X – Pickfords, 60, Long Lane, SE1

82U – Alma School, Southward Park Road, SE1

Short Index